THE KEY TO HEAVEN

by
May Clark

CON-PSY PUBLICATIONS MIDDLESEX

First Edition

© May Clark
2006

Published by

CON-PSY PUBLICATIONS

P.O. BOX 14,
GREENFORD,
MIDDLESEX, UB6 0UF.

ISBN 1 898680 41 8
ISBN 978 1 898680 41 3

Index

FOREWORD

This is the second volume of inspirational writings received by my friend, May Clark, from her beloved Spirit Guide, Pharaoh.

Pharaoh is a highly evolved soul seeking to bring God's truth to help humanity as it struggles through the vicissitudes of the earthly life, In May, he has been fortunate to find a channel of exceptional spiritual clarity through whose mediumship his message can be conveyed with total accuracy.

May's first volume of writings (Teachings of Infinite Wisdom) came from Pharaoh and her guide, Ming Fu, and the spiritual food and knowledge contained therein has found wide favour, helping many souls along the way. It is widely read in Spiritualist churches and in Home Circles.

I have no doubt that this companion volume will find equal favour and will continue to help seekers in the years to come.

Teresa Doherty
St Leonards-on-Sea

PHARAOH

Spirit Guide of May Clark
Illustration by Marie Armstrong

POWER OF DIVINITY

They who draw unto themselves the power of the spirit will indeed meet and overcome the difficulties of life in a positive way, For they shall be aware of the light of inspiration guiding them.

So much can be gained by allowing the power of the spirit to come into your life. It flows in abundance from the Father of all, and it is thus up to His children as to whether or not we partake of it.

We in Spirit are only too well aware of the many souls in your world who do not invite God into their lives, which alas leaves the spark of divine light within their being dim indeed, for it cannot shine forth brightly from them until their heart welcomes Him.

Each and every child of the Great Spirit is blessed with free will, so whichever path you choose to take in life will be your responsibility. Therefore, I say to you, give careful consideration to the seeds you plant along the way. Bear in mind your thoughts, deeds and actions will have a bearing on the seeds you sow. See then they are good ones and thus, by doing so, the harvest you reap shall be a rewarding one.

They who try to live their life in a wholesome way, allowing spiritual truths to guide them, are wise indeed, for they shall gain much that will be of immense value to their spirit.

Those who take the path that satisfies only the material aspect of their being will arrive in Spirit World one day with nothing of worth to show their Father God. What a sad state of affairs this will be. What is more, their soul shall show a marked deficiency of those nutrients which have been denied it, because things material were given preference over the good food of the spirit which should be seen as so necessary for the encouragement of sound growth.

More and more, we see souls falling by the wayside, mainly due to the fact that they are without eternal truths to guide them, which prevents them from moving into the light of understanding where they could rise above the ignorance which leaves so many of God's children in a state of disarray.

If man is to grow in spiritual awareness, then he must seek out that which could be beneficial to him. Sadly, numerous souls in your world are festering in a role of discontentment because their soul is unfulfilled. Remember, beloved ones, life holds many good and interesting things to help mankind prosper in a spiritual way. Why not make use of them? They cost nothing but your time to discover them, which could be so worthwhile as you would see.

May the wisdom I bring give you the incentive to go forth on the path of spiritual unfoldment where the power of the spirit moves you closer to God. Glories await the aspirant soul who wants to reach the summit of spirituality. Be then one of those who are striving to achieve this ideal.

ON WINGS OF LOVE

There are so many words of truth being sent out to your world on wings of love from my side of life. Allow me to impart mine too that you might in some way derive benefit from them.

Truth is the gem one should treasure, For without it one cannot enter the door of realisation. If our mind is to awaken to what really matters then we must allow truth and that of knowledge to guide us. Spiritual progression cannot be made without them, as they hold the light which beckons us on to gain the opportunity to soar to Heaven's gate.

Alas, your world holds numerous souls who shun the Fact that another world awaits them when their earth life is spent, and thus they fail to prepare for that journey ahead. Sadly, when the time comes For them to embark on this,their state of mind will block the way forward. Bewilderment shall be their lot to experience until they are ready to learn what they unwisely turned away From.

Beings who have lived their lives wisely and thus have taken the time to educate themselves with spiritual matters shall find they are well equipped to step forward into the next life with ease, to therefore go Forth to enjoy the great adventure awaiting them.

Much awaits those who are spiritually motivated. Gaining the Fruits of the spirit will not be hard to achieve, for they will see clearly how to work towards those things holding so much goodness that can help their soul to grow strong. The progress your soul makes depends on the education it receives. If it is sound in every sense of the word, then you can be sure that graduation to higher dimensions will take place. If our soul is to radiate the light of God, then we must endeavour to live and work in a way He would approve of.

So many beings are not playing Fair in life, they abuse all God stands For, His laws are not being obeyed and respect it appears is thin on the ground, which shows us a very sad picture indeed. Sooner or later, mankind will be obliged to face up to the fact that if the world is to revert from the dire state it is in, then a change in his way of thinking must come about. He needs to understand that grasping for material things the way he does will not bring him true contentment which his soul yearns For.

Much greed and selfishness is being shown in many lives which cannot possibly encourage soul growth. Man can show such foolishness at times in the way he conducts his life. Rarely is it founded on wisdom, this is why complications arise to thus create the unrest he so often experiences. The sooner man gains victory over ignorance the sooner his spiritual progression can take shape.

Through aeons of time man has clouded the atmosphere around him by unkind thoughts and deeds which appear to be on the increase as he allows

7

his lower self to dominate.

We try to make you aware of the mistakes you are making that you might rectify them, but if you fail to heed our words we have no choice but to leave you to learn the hard way.

So many words of truth are sent to you on wings of love, but sadly they do not always take root in your mind to inspire you as they should because a barrier is set up against them. Bear in mind, children of the Great Spirit, you have nothing to lose by listening to us. Indeed, you have much to gain by opening your mind to what we bring. Allow God's light to shine through your lives and you will not lose touch with what truly matters.

THE FABRIC OF YOUR LIFE

Build into the fabric of your life that which comes From a spiritual source, for it holds what you need to help you gain strength of character, which is so important if one is to advance towards the Godhead.

We are aware of so many in your world who are not at all interested in improving their characteristics by allowing truth to guide them. Wise indeed are they who allow the gems of knowledge to enter their mind, for they are at least showing interest.

God grants to us, His children, the gift of wisdom that it might accompany us as we travel life's way, but alas so few use it. If they did so, your world would show a much different picture than it does today. Lack of wisdom is distinctly shown in the chaotic conditions sadly prevailing, and until Man sees with clear vision the reason for that which has come about, nothing will change. Indeed, problems shall continue to increase, creating further chaos.

If only Man would seek to learn the full facts of life relating to the laws governing the universe, he would see where he is going wrong and amendments could then be made.

There is without doubt a goodly number of souls living on the earth plane who flounder in the wake of ignorance. If they would only reach out for the light of understanding that all can enter into, they would see the right way to live. The enlightened mind knows there is only one sure way to travel to find the gateway to greater things, and that is through service which one can carry out in many ways.

Every moment of time counts where your spiritual education is concerned. There is much waiting to be learnt which your soul depends upon for its graduation to higher dimensions. Without life's vital knowledge to guide us, progress cannot be made. Search out and use those things holding the golden threads of spirituality. By weaving them into the fabric of your life, your spirit will shine before God and this, beloved ones, is what He yearns to see.

8

THE TRUTH AND THE LIGHT

Both of these things are what you need if you want to travel the path of spiritual progression. Truth releases one from the bondage of ignorance, thus allowing us to enter the light of understanding where the meaning of life becomes clearer to us, enabling one to put into perspective that which truly matters.

The pearls of truth and the power of the light can, without doubt, enhance our spirituality. They allow us to gain entry to higher dimensions where greater knowledge prevails.

They who base their lives on truth, knowledge and wisdom cannot fall to progress towards the glory of God, because all hold the key to His heart. Furthermore, if you want peace and harmony to flow through what you do, then you should conduct your lives to the tune of the spirit, which is not difficult once you learn the art of it.

Praise be to those who take upon themselves the work of the spirit, for they truly carry out tasks of a worthwhile kind and thus they are blessed for what they do. Willing helpers are always in great demand and we in Spirit are so thankful for them.

Sharing and caring are the most benevolent things, and we know the Great Spirit smiles upon those who show they are loving givers, who expect no reward for services rendered. So powerful is the light of God, we are so conscious of His Presence which upholds us in all that we do for Him. Many of the tasks we take on need the strength of His being to bear upon us, such as when we are faced with trying to free souls from the dark forces of life which they have allowed to corrupt their spirit.

This can be a most difficult undertaking which calls for strength, patience and that of determination to win through. Sadly, some are held fast by evil which is a most unpleasant sight to see. However, our perseverance in trying to release them must not wane, even though it might take a long duration of time.

Again and again, we may need to offer them the torch of truth to help them see the way to move forward into the light of goodness awaiting them. Thus, it is a wonderful experience when we gain victory, but then our aim is to settle for nothing less.

Beloved ones, we who are mentors come to teach you the basic facts of life that you might use them to build a strong foundation for your soul growth. In the light of what we bring, you can be sure it holds the truth of that which your soul needs to encourage it to blossom beautifully.

THE GOOD SHEPHERD

To those who are lost in life, lonely, or in despair, I say to you, think of the Good Shepherd who awaits to guide you, if you would but only ask Him the way.

Remember, beloved ones, there is a lot mankind could learn from His teachings. The words He spoke hold truth and wisdom which shall never die; they are printed on the ether of life for all time.

No soul need be starved of knowledge. The Good Shepherd supplied much to feed the mind of Man that he might thrive spiritually. Refreshment of this nourishment can always be partaken of, if one is prepared to seek it.

The Good Shepherd, Who watches over humanity, works constantly for the betterment of the world, which is indeed in a dire state of turmoil which stems from Man's ignorance. His task could be made easy if only mankind would take steps to enlighten themselves with the full facts of life. But, alas, many would rather muddle their way through life in an ignorant fashion, breeding trouble for themselves, and others too.

We pity those who live this way, for the spiritual aspect of their being is so neglected. Sadly, their soul will show stunted growth, thus revealing how foolishly they have lived their life.

The beauty emanating from one's soul will depend entirely on how spiritually we are living, and this is what God looks for when choosing channels for His work. Brightly shines the light from those who work in all sincerity for the Great Spirit, for the rays they draw unto themselves shall be of the purest kind, thus giving radiance to their being.

Alas, there are a great number of God's children who profess to work for Him wholeheartedly, but they cannot hide the tell-tale light surrounding them, which denotes the truth of what they do. It shows us clearly the sham or the genuineness of their actions. They who are deceitful could not possibly derive true satisfaction from what they do, as they are not working within God's laws and thus would be frowned upon by Him Most High.

Golden opportunities, however, come to those who show they are sincere and dedicated workers, for they shall have placed before them privileged tasks which can indeed enable them to move more swiftly towards reaching that state of consciousness where wise ones dwell,to thus receive greater knowledge which could strengthen the threads of their work.

The Good Shepherd looks to those He knows are worthy channels to help Him with His work. There is a lot to be done if your world if it's to be lifted out of the quandary it is in. Much darkness prevails, due to Man's unwise way of living. Children of God, you are facing such heartache if you allow the state of your planet to continue as it is. We see chaos in plenty, preventing the light of peace and harmony and that of goodness from entering in.

Man must learn to listen to reason and understand too that he is responsible for the role he plays in life. If he chooses to act irresponsibility, then sooner or later he must face the consequences of his contemptible actions, which he shall not by any means find easy.

To those of you who have gathered wisdom to you in your search for truth, I say go forward, beloved ones, and pass on what you have gained to others in need. Help them to become enlightened so that more light can be created in the world where it might reign over that which is being allowed to destroy what the Father God so trustfully put in our care.

THE GARDEN OF YOUR SOUL

Plant the seeds of love, peace and goodwill in the garden of your soul that they might germinate and thus produce a wealth of loveliness as they blossom from the goodness you have sown. More than ever, it seems, man must be encouraged to be aware of how imperative it is to grow seeds of benevolence in his life to help him evolve in a superior way.

So many in your world are sowing seeds of destruction from wrong thinking, which is very sad to see. Man should tend the garden of his soul with care, allowing only that to grow which can be productive to him. He must weed out what could be harmful to his growth and so leave space for the planting of seeds that would bring a profitable return.

Alas, ignorance is the blight of man's life, and thus can distort what should be lovely in God's sight. Foolish is he who fails to learn the correct way of cultivation, for he could be left with poor growth.

God's children should bear in mind that He supplies them with the tools of wisdom to help them create good conditions in their lives. But sadly so few use them, and thus find life a complicated affair. You do well to remember you are responsible for the way your life takes shape, and thus should take care in thought, word and deed, for all shall reflect on the image you display on the other side of life. So, I say to those of you who are neglecting what should be important to you, take stock of all that needs to be rectified and thus see that it is put right.

Beloved ones, it is with God's blessing I bring truth to bear upon you that you might gain wisdom from what I have said. So ponder upon the words I have spoken for they could feed the needs of your soul, and forget not this, that they who sow seeds of goodness shall indeed reap a fine harvest. Tend then the garden of your soul with care and may all you grow there be truly wonderful to see.

11

THE WAY TO GOD'S HEART

It is by striving to reach perfection that one finds the way to God's heart. I therefore beseech thee to go forward and seek the knowledge that could help to set you on course to Him Who reigns most high.

The path to the Giver of Life, however, is not an easy one to follow, but if you want to develop the finer side of your being, to be with Him in the fullness of time, then you must be prepared to be steadfast through the trials of the spirit which are essential to your inner growth. But bear in mind this, beloved ones, so much can be gained by pursuing this path of immense opportunity, for it allows one to capture prime truth that enriches the soul, helping it to ascend to higher dimensions where God's bright ones dwell. These beings of the light are privileged to guide you for they have endeavoured to reach this stage of enlightenment through a long period of learning and so, with God's blessing, they gladly impart knowledge gained to aid your progress.

We see so many beings in your world fritter their time away by pursuing that which can bring them material gain, but this will not satisfy their spirit which longs for fulfilment from things of a spiritual kind.

Try to weave into your life the golden threads of spirituality which can strengthen and give brightness to your soul that you might be an inspiration to others who might be encouraged to do likewise.

Beloved ones, there are many ways in which one can find the way to God's heart, but, whatever one you choose, see that it is founded on good principles which must be a major factor in your life.

How sad it is that so many of God's children show no interest in wanting to know Him and thus they wonder why their life seems like an empty shell. They need to learn that by shutting out their Creator they prevent the warmth of His love from coming through, which could so uplift and inspire the heart of their being.

Blessed are they who want to know Him and who indeed want to serve Him in whatever way they can, and it matters not whether the task be great or small, all are appreciated and are recorded on the higher side of life. They who are dedicated shall find a wonderful reception awaits them, for God does not overlook what is done in His Name and thus shows His gratitude in full measure.

God is the Great One of the Universe. All things are made possible through Him. Never doubt His wisdom, one day you shall know the true nature of Him, which in your present state you cannot truly comprehend. But know this, He is a most loving Father. Be then faithful to His Name.

IN TUNE WITH GOD

Not many, it appears, are in tune with God. If they were so their lives would be more harmonious. Again and again we see souls acting against the laws of life, which only creates problems. When will Mankind see wisdom in working with God, instead of opposing what He wants us to respect. Indeed, Mankind has much to learn about life and its purpose.

Sadly, your world holds a goodly number of beings who remain in a state of slumber, oblivious to what life is about. Some simply do not want to know and thus close their minds to what we try to teach them. Ignorance is, without doubt, the root cause of the world's problems and will continue to be Man's stumbling block until enlightenment is gained.

Materialism ranks far too high in the lives of many and thus it seems, the more in the way of the material they have, the more they want. Rarely do the things they obtain from their craving bring any true satisfaction. The reason for this stems from the fact that, because they are allowing the material to be too dominant in their lives, the spiritual aspect of their being is having to suffer the consequences of this action, for it becomes neglected, which results in disharmony taking place.

Thus, it stands to reason, how can any satisfaction be truly experienced when an imbalance has been created by this foolish way of living. If they were wise in their way of thinking, material gain would be seen in a different light, one that shows how valueless this is against that of the spirit.

It is most unwise to set great store by things which hold no true value. Regret could be yours one day if you do. Bear in mind, beloved ones, nothing of the material can be carried with you when your Father God calls you back home to Spirit. All you take is your character and what you have gained spiritually.

Enjoy the things of the material by all means, but place them not above the spiritual. Avoid wasting time in pandering to the whims of the lower self. Put your time to good use by doing things your higher self could benefit from. There is wisdom in this.

If you want to be in tune with God, then first and foremost you must see your lives are based on good principles. Respect, too, His Creation, even though you may not understand the reason for some of the things created. One should try to accept there is a purpose behind what we see, and one day, in God's good time, He will see fit to enlighten us on those things which appear perplexing to us.

Those who are disrupting your planet earth by their callous behaviour need to wake up to the fact that what they are doing will get them nowhere, other than to help them to sink lower and lower into the pit of destruction, which I can assure you is a most unpleasant sight to see.

13

It is so true that Man can be his own worst enemy. Because he falls to listen to reason, the difficulties he creates in his life tend to backfire on him. If he would only learn to conduct His life in the correct manner, he would avoid the heartache his lack of wisdom brings.

Remember, your soul's progress is in your hands. Do not prevent it by being out of tune with God,The Great One of All, and the rhythm running through all of life.

SERVANTS OF THE LIGHT

Ye who have chosen to serve the Great Spirit shall indeed walk in the radiance of His love, because you draw unto yourselves the closeness of His being.

The path of service can be a difficult one to follow, for the tests of the spirit are many, subjecting one to much soul searching. Thus, only those who are strong in spirit shall prove to be true servants of the light.

Work for the Divine One should never be taken lightly. The tasks He giveth unto you hold responsibility and therefore must be carried out in a just and caring way. The pattern of your life should be one that shows dedication woven with love, which comes from a heart that is true. Time and time again you could be asked to help those less strong in spirit who have not yet mastered the calling of the lower mind, thus the knowledge you impart to these unenlightened ones must be chosen with care if they are to gain insight into the higher truths of life.

Bear in mind, beloved ones, you hold the torch of truth and so are privileged to show others the way. Therefore, do not discredit this by failing to apply thoughtfulness to those who are blind to the reality of life. Beings such as these need to be gently awakened to that which is vital to their progress. Nothing can be gained by forcing knowledge on to others who are not yet ready to receive it, as this would only blight the good you try to do.

Many servants of the light are followers of the Christ Spirit and thus are influenced by His teachings, which are so wise and therefore are acceptable in every way. This fine being, who serves God from the highest point of spirituality, knows only too well the plight your world is in, brought about by man's irresponsible behaviour, lack of insight, greed for gain, and desire for power over others. Some even try to play at being God. But the time will surely come when man must change his way of thinking to thus help him to move towards the light of understanding.

To those of you who have reached this level of consciousness and have pledged service to God, I say to you, go forth and teach mankind the true way to live, to help them rise above that which could pull them down into the pit of destruction.

14

SPIRITUAL GROWTH

Beloved ones, allow your spiritual growth to be fortified with the good food of the spirit, which can be found in the great storehouse of life.

They who seek to find that which their soul hungers for shall discover in the wake of their searching many things containing the nutrients so essential to the sound functioning of the mind, soul and spirit. The Great Father provides well for His children, but alas so few appreciate what He gives and thus are inclined to foolishly turn away from that which could be important to them.

Souls such as these often find they are without the stamina to help them overcome the trials and tribulations of life, because their staying power has not been reinforced with that vital stimulus which is that of knowledge.

Time and time again, man fails to see the wisdom in supplying his mind with the truth of that which truly matters in life. Far too many souls are more than content to drift through life in a negative way, giving no thought to the spiritual aspect of their being; but, if it is to eventually reach a perfected state, then it must mature in the light of all that is fundamental to its growth.

Alas, there are those of God's children who tend to overlook the fact that the time shall come when their physical body will have served its purpose, thus allowing the soul within freedom to journey back home to Spirit, where a viewing of the earth life must be met. Nothing is hidden from the beholder, for it is imperative all is seen in the light of truth, to thus enable the soul to view with clarity the progress that has been made.

Those souls who have achieved much spiritually, can expect to go forward to gain from the good they have sown. But should selfishness and greed, and that of irresponsibility, have been given dominance over spiritual matters, then the soul would have created a stumbling block from such things, which prevents it from moving towards those realms of wonder.

The removal of such an obstruction comes from the soul's decision to change its way of thinking, by seeing how infertile this behaviour can be, for no good growth nor progress can come from it. Sadly, we often see many who stubbornly refuse to see reason, and who prefer to go on in the same old way, and so we must leave them to their own devices until such a time comes when they see the error of their way, and realise too that their unwholesome way of living does nothing but cast dark shadows around them.

Wise is he who reaches out for the riches of the spirit, for these things can adorn one's soul and without doubt meet with the Great Father's full approval.

Beloved ones, I beseech thee to bear in mind that which has been revealed to you in all truth, because it could help to strengthen your spiritual

15

growth. Try then to put into practice the way of the spirit, and thus you can take joy from knowing that the beauty from your blossoming soul shall indeed be given pride of place in God's great tapestry.

IN THE LIGHT OF KNOWLEDGE

There is much to be gained when one becomes immersed in the light of knowledge. What we learn can, without doubt, take us further up the stairway of life to experience greater things which God has in store For us, and we can be sure many, many treasures await us if we show our Father in all sincerity that we desire to reach the glory of where He dwells.

We know the perfected state aimed for will not be an easy one to achieve, but if we truly want to accomplish this, then we must practise the way of the Master who had no doubt about the route that should be taken to reach such a cherished goal so dreamed of.

Opportunity to progress comes to all God's children. There is no favouritism where He is concerned, all receive in equal measure His care and attention for their soul development.

The state of the world might belie the fact that God is a loving Father, so many of His children are suffering in some way or another, but, beloved ones, the plight these souls are in is so often of their own making, simply because they have not complied with the laws of life. What is more, the turning away from opportunities granted to them from God's great storehouse could also be the reason why their lives are in turmoil.

So much of what you see is of mankind's own making, and thus Man must suffer the consequences of his actions. It is indeed wrong to blame God for the chaos caused by one's irresponsibility. Man should look within himself and weed out those things which create trouble and strife for himself, and others too.

You are all capable of contributing something good to the world, no matter how small it might be. It all helps to create light which the world needs in plenty. Your Earth Planet portrays a very sad picture indeed. Doom and gloom spreads rapidly because so many are allowing dark deeds and desires to taint God's wonderful universe, thus casting shadows where light should be. Thankfully, there are those beings who show a bright shining spirit, who give to the world the best they can. This helps to dispel the grey mist Formed by those who are of a lower nature.

Dear children of the Great Spirit, cast the seeds of loving kindness where'er you go to sweeten the atmosphere of life. Remember, good seeds planted can bring about fine results, which the Divine One will bless you for.

THE LORD GIVETH

We who work closely with The Lord know how much He giveth to humanity. But, alas, it saddens our hearts when we see so few responding to what He wants mankind to achieve.

The fact of the matter is, mankind has become more and more materialistic. The state of your world shows all too clearly the result of this. However, in spite of those who are indifferent to what He gives, He continues to pour forth light, love and peace in full measure, trusting as He does so that Man might be touched by this and thus become inspired to take the path of righteousness where soul promotion can be gained by what is learnt on the way.

The Lord works tirelessly for the good of the world which, believe me, is no easy task. He is dealing with such chaotic conditions that are difficult to solve when the minds of mankind refuse to listen to reason.

There are those on the earth plane who are bent on destroying God's creation. Their hearts are cold, and it matters not to them who they hurt in the process of what they do. What a rude awakening awaits them one day when their life on earth is spent.

If Man wants to walk in the light of goodness then his aim must be to learn the full facts of life which teach the right way to live. To muddle his way through life without directions will only create problems for him. He must carry the torch of truth to help him see the way to go.

Remember, beloved ones, the wise man will at all times keep company with truth, knowledge and wisdom, for they are, without doubt, the main threesome he needs to guide him. We know life can be an uphill climb which so often bring weariness in its wake, but in our heart of hearts we know we must continue to move on and try to accept those things which test one's spirit. They are, after all, blessings in disguise and they enable our soul to mature, which is so necessary if it is to reach the source of all life.

The Lord, Who giveth of Himself to help mankind moved closer to God, learnt, too, how difficult it is to pass through the traumas of life showing courage, stamina and goodwill. The Lord knew His work for God, The Father, was a mission He had undertaken to do. To call defeat when the going was tough would have gone against the grain of what He taught, which He had no intention of jeopardising, for His love for His Father and humanity was too great to allow this to happen.

The Lord asks nothing in return for what He giveth. All He wants to see is His brethren working together in love and harmony, so that brighter conditions might prevail in the world. You can all make this come to pass by playing a good role in life. Look around you and you will find many in need of friendship. Some yearn for comfort in times of despair.

There are numerous things waiting to be done to help your world become a better place to live in. Furthermore, why not follow the Lord's code of conduct. No wiser Teacher could you find. His teachings mean the same today as they did all those years ago, and thus shall forever be Man's guiding light.

WALK IN THE RAINBOW OF LIFE

Allow me to guide you into the light that is all good, powerful and kind and you shall find your life takes on a new meaning which secures you in the knowledge that you have found oneness with God.

So many of you are like empty vessels that need to be filled with inspiration to help you create good things in your life. Therefore, it is my aim to bring you a goodly measure of that which might permit you to see how satisfactory your life could be by fulfiling the needs of your soul.

Try not to waste your life by pursuing that which offers no scope for developing the finer points of your being. You do well to remember it is a wise man who gathers to himself wisdom, truth and knowledge, for they shall prove to be the mainstay of his life and thus will always serve him well.

To those who want to walk in the rainbow of life, I say to you, endeavour to enrich your soul with the things of the spirit, for by doing so you shall emanate rays of coloured lights from you which will enhance the whole of your being. Sadly, there are many in your world who are heading for a rude awakening, because they believe the earth life is the be-all and end-all of existence, thus their way of life is more often than not one that is steeped in the material.

I cannot over-emphasise how important it is that you seek to learn what is on the other side of the coin of life, because you would then see and thus realise how essential spiritual education is, for your soul cannot develop constructively without it.

You should not place material values above those of the spirit in any shape or form, because you would eventually find you have nothing to take with you when that call comes for you to return home to Spirit. Remember, your life on the earth plane is relatively short when compared with your future life in Spirit World, and so with wisdom you must try to enlighten your mind with knowledge which can prepare you for residence in that future state.

Bear in mind, beloved ones, much can be gained by endeavouring to use your time in gathering spiritual truths, for thus by doing so you shall hold something very precious which in turn can be used to help guide others as you travel forth on life's way.

THE GOLDEN THREADS OF SPIRITUALITY

Children of the Great Spirit, I say to you, weave into your life the golden threads of spirituality to strengthen the fabric of your being.

So many of you lose faith in Him who loves you when the trials and tribulations of life are hard to bear, but one must remember that, with each problem life deals out, there is a lesson to be learnt to help you gain insight into the reality of life, which otherwise might not be fully understood. Wise are they who accept their difficulties in a rational way, for they shall flow with the tide of life, knowing as they do so they are accepting what comes to test their spirit, instead of fighting against it.

Opportunity to advance to a greater height of learning will come throughout your life, but many of you are likely to turn away from that which invites you to do so, and thus vital steps forward could be lost. Bear in mind, beloved ones, nothing ventured, nothing gained.

Your path in life could be an adventurous one, if you would only seek to learn spiritual truths, for this could lead you to undertake work for God, where many avenues of service open up to you. Much awaits those who venture forth to gain a higher degree of spirituality, because God shall place before them many interesting things to help them progress and so achieve that which their soul seeks.

Sadly, there are a large number of beings in your world who do nothing to improve their spiritual education, and thus fail to enrich their spirit with what could draw it closer to God.

We, from the higher planes of Spirit World, have learnt much by our willingness to strive through numerous heartfelt experiences to gain the knowledge we need to help lift your world from the darkness that prevails, brought about by man's ignorance and his unhealthy way of living. But, alas, until mankind is ready to listen to the truth we bring and is prepared to learn from the mistakes they have made, we cannot help them move into the light that awaits them.

Man needs to put more value on creating those things that are essential in bringing about peace and harmony. He needs to place importance too on learning the art of goodwill, which is often sadly lacking in your world. Man must try to get a balance in his life by learning facts from both worlds. This would help him see things in perspective and thus he could put right that which is wrong.

What is more, he could do no better than to weave into his life the golden threads of spirituality, for not only will they strengthen the fabric of his being but they shall help him to shine before God.

UNTO HIM BE TRUE

Children of the Great Spirit, be true unto Him, the Creator of your being, and allow His light to guide you in all that you do. Never doubt the strength of His power, nor the wisdom He holds. Remember, He Who is your loving Father knows what is best for you, and thus you should bear this in mind when things do not always work out in accordance with your plans. It could mean He has intervened, saving you from a situation that would not be right for the rhythm of your progress.

Although unseen, we can be sure His Spirit is close to us. They who take time to meditate, in the true sense of the word, shall indeed feel His Presence as He allows the love and peace He holds to flow through their being.

It is during these times of quietude one is more conscious of their spirit blending with that of the Divine One. Sadly, your world holds a great number of beings who show no respect for God, nor indeed for His creation. They allow their lower self to dominate their lives in a most shameful way, often bent on destroying. They show no remorse for the chaos that is created by their thoughtlessness.

However, the day shall come when they must face retribution, thus from their own making they will find themselves in a state of darkness. No light shall they see until their mind registers regret, then and only then will the light appear to help guide them forward, where opportunity is given to thus enable them to put right what they have done wrong.

We teachers of truth cannot stress too strongly how important it is to refrain from breaking the laws of life. The enlightened man knows the consequences of what happens when he does so, and therefore is careful in the way he conducts his life.

We urge those of God's children who are ignorant of the true facts of life to seek enlightenment. Spiritual education is so vital to one's graduation to higher levels of consciousness, where greater knowledge lies which can help us to move further and further up the stairway of life until we at last reach the Supreme Spirit of love Whose light we shall be engulfed in.

We know that life, with all its mysteries, cannot be rightly understood. God holds much to Him which He knows we are not ready to receive. The jigsaw of life is therefore given to us, piece by piece, until He sees fit to show us the whole picture of life. Till then we must keep faith in knowing our lives are being directed in a sure and steady way towards the glory of what has been planned for us.

Do not spoil this by taking the path that could lead to self-destruction because you think your way is best. Believe me, you stand to lose much that your spirit yearns for. Deprive it not of that which it needs.

ENLIGHTENMENT

The way to enlightenment is not hard to find if your heart is in what you are seeking, for they who truly seek to learn that which can help them become spiritually aware shall without doubt be guided to discover the knowledge their soul needs.

The Great Spirit wants to see His children develop a keen interest in the spiritual aspect of their being, so that they might understand how important it is to cultivate good sound growth which the soul depends upon if it is to function in a satisfactory way.

They who are enlightened know the way to progression and thus endeavour to put into practice what enables them to advance towards the light of Him Who is all powerful and kind. To those who live in the shadows of doubt because they are not in receipt of what is vital to the development of their soul, I say to them, waste not another moment of time by delaying the search for truth; every second counts where one's spiritual growth is concerned.

There are many things in life one can draw enlightenment from to open up awareness to what really matters. Alas, many beings live in a state of slumber, oblivious of the fact that they are on the earth plane for a purpose. Regrettably, there is little aid we can give them until they show signs of awakening to reality, which in some cases could take a good deal of time.

We from the higher side of life implore you to be more far-seeing in the matter of your progress, because the rate of this will determine your soul's place of residence in the greater world to come.

We know the cares of the earth plane are many, which does not make for contented living, but one must bear in mind there is a reason for all things, and if your attitude be one where you appreciate this, then this will help you to take them in your stride. The spirit of Man must be tested time and time again in the furnace of life's experiences to thus enable it to become strong in every sense of the word.

The spirit of many is weak and therefore needs to be strengthened by methods God sees fit to send it, but this could prove to be lengthy, depending on how the spirit responds to what is trying to bring about good results.

The nature of Man is such that he can so easily overlook the important factors of life essential to his progress. More often than not, he allows himself to be swayed too much towards the material, which then leaves the spiritual aspect of his being in a state of neglect, thus creating an unbalance in the stem of his growth.

The need for enlightenment in your world is becoming more and more crucial, for as we view all that has arisen from Man's ignorance, we know there is much to be eradicated. For too long the laws of life have been ignored by many, which has created the chaos seen today. If Man is to banish the doom and gloom that prevails, then he must start to put the world to rights by seeking knowledge that can help him.

Beloved ones, I beseech thee to face the truth I bring. To shy away from what is vital to your soul's education would be unwise indeed. We try to guide your footsteps in the right direction but, of course, it rests with you as to whether or not you choose to walk the way of the Spirit. But, remember the enlightened mind gains much and thus is a happy one.

THE SHACKLES OF IGNORANCE

Ye who are held in the shackles of ignorance hearken to my words, for they could help to free you from that which binds you to thus enable you to journey through life in a progressive way.

Enlightenment keeps one aloft, helping us to see where we are heading to claim the prize of life. Without this to guide us, we stand to lose our sense of direction and become lost in a state of confusion, wondering what life is about.

So many of God's children are in a state of disarray because they refuse to listen to reason. They fret and fume about things which could be avoided if seen in a different light. Knowledge is what they need to enable them to understand the truth of life. Once they hold the key to this, progress can be made.

We know there is a lot to learn about life, but if we do not take the trouble to search for the knowledge we need to broaden our understanding, how can we expect to be free from ignorance. It rests with us, beloved ones, to seek the answers to what perplexes us. Guidance will always be forthcoming if we show sincerity, for the wise ones in Spirit will indeed light up truth for us to see when we strive to learn it.

Alas, there are they who show no interest in the spiritual aspect of things, believing the material is all that matters. Such beings are neglecting the vital part of them, which is very sad to see. We ask you to think carefully over what you do in your lives, because the seeds you sow from what you carry out will determine the harvest you reap in your next stage of existence.

If you want to reap a fine harvest, avoid living in a careless fashion. Try to be of service to others. Take time to listen and guide those in need. Develop good qualities by practising the way of the spirit. Put your time to good use, do not allow idleness to entertain you. There is much work to be done in your world to clear the darkness that prevails. Try to create more light by being a worthy citizen, doing only that which is right.

Furthermore, conquer the encumbrance of ignorance by reaching out for enlightenment, and you will be in a better position to thus achieve the fine goals of life.

THE TESTS OF LIFE

The tests of life come in many guises and thus we cannot tell when or how they are likely to manifest in our lives. So, the best policy to take is one whereby we see trials and tribulations as challenges we must endeavour to gain victory over if we are to grow spiritually strong.

Life can be a hard taskmaster. Some of the experiences one might encounter could prove to be difficult indeed, but understand this, beloved ones, whatever life deals out, we can be sure it holds a lesson for us to learn from.

Alas, your world teems with souls who are totally ignorant of the true facts of life, and therefore are inclined to make the same mistakes time and time again, which of course delays their soul development. Thus, it is with concern, I appeal to those of you who are enlightened to give of your time to thus help beings such as these to become aware of life's important factors so that they, too, might make progress towards the light, where He Who is all powerful dwells.

Remember, beloved ones, your Father God wants you to share what knowledge you have acquired with others who could be in need of this. To keep it solely to yourselves for your own satisfaction would be wrong. There are many wanting ones in your world who long for enlightenment, be then their guiding light by bringing truth to bear upon them, thus helping them to gain insight into those things which could be perplexing to them.

They who awaken to the truth of the Spirit shall indeed find their life taking on a new meaning, as they begin to view things in a different light. That of the material shall not have the same magnetic draw for them, because their heightened awareness will allow them to see where the best values lie. However, it is important one learns from both worlds, both hold educational worth which we need to help us form an all round picture of things.

The Great Father wants His children to become educationally sound in every way, so that the role of mastership might be theirs one day, and this can be achieved, have no doubt about that, for did not Jesus the Christ, and many others, reach this ideal. But one must, however, be prepared to strive steadfastly towards reaching this goal with fortitude. Many tests will need to be endured, for one must prove to be strong in mind and spirit to thus warrant such a high ranking position.

Throughout life, every child of God is given opportunity to move further and Further up the ladder of life to reach higher levels of consciousness, until they eventually earn the right to join forces with those who have gained the Great Father's trust in every sense of the word.

Sadly, many souls show indifference to that which comes to aid them, which prevents them from gaining spiritual maturity. But, we pray these ones shall awaken to the foolishness of their actions and thus start to realise the truth of what lies in those opportunities God sends us for our progress' sake.

I trust the message I bring will light up your life, helping you to see how wise it is to pass through the tests of life with courage and goodwill, knowing that by doing so much shall be gained in your favour.

TIME IS PRECIOUS

Waste not your lives in useless pursuits. Time is precious and therefore should be used in ways that spur on your spiritual growth, which after all is the most vital part of you.

Ye children of the Earth Plane can be so materialistic, whereby the spiritual aspect of your being becomes neglected and thus your soul's development suffers the consequences of this.

God the Father understands that, whilst His children live on a material plane, things of a material nature must be catered for, but not, I hasten to add, to the extent where one's spirituality is overlooked or cast aside as if of no importance. Be wise and try to obtain a balance so that both function satisfactorily on an even keel.

Such a large majority live only for material gain, often using methods to achieve what they want which the Father frowns upon. This type of individual has much to learn and thus shall realise one day how unwise they have been. We say to you, live your lives in the light of those things containing the essence of goodness, that they might beautify your soul.

Life offers much to help you grow spiritually strong. By seeking out what could aid your progress, your soul will find joy in the wake of this, for it would be gaining that which it needs to promote it forward.

Remember, beloved ones, knowledge holds the key to advancement. Therefore, one should make sure of gaining this if headway is to be made. Alas, your world teems with beings who fritter their lives away in an idle fashion. If only they would realise how precious time is and thus try to put it to good use, what a difference this would make to the growth and strength of their spirit, which always benefits from the worthwhile things we do, and God is ever conscious of this, for nothing escapes His eye.

The mighty hand of God blesses all whom He sees working towards reaching the summit of spirituality. He knows this is not easy because of the many tests one meets along the way. To keep on the straight and narrow takes courage, stamina and goodwill, but they who are enlightened know all that is endured works out well worth while in the end.

BLESSED ARE THEY

Blessed are they whose way of life meets with God's approval, for they shall draw around themselves the radiance of His light.

The Great Father's desire is to see His children working towards gaining a higher degree of spirituality to enable their souls to mature and thus graduate to that dimension where love, light and power are greater by far than one can imagine. It is in this state of consciousness that the spirit becomes aware of God's embrace as it is blessed for all that has been achieved. No greater joy can one claim than that of ascending to this realm which holds so much wondrous beauty, for it echoes all God stands for, thus making one truly aware of how great He is.

But, one must remember, progress towards the Source of all life depends very much on one's willingness to meet and overcome the tests of the spirit which are essential for soul growth. They who are determined to make strides forward, come what may, shall find they are given the strength and courage to overcome what tries to defeat them, because the Great Father giveth unto those who show strength of purpose the power to make headway.

To those who are drifting through life in a negative way, I say to you, waste not what your Father has blessed you with, for within your being lies creative ability which should be encouraged to find expression in some shape or form where it can be used for the good of the world.

They who take time to discover and bring to the fore what lies within shall indeed find their life takes on a new meaning, because inspiration will move them to put into operation that which could be of fine value.

Your world,beloved ones,sadly holds numerous souls who are neglecting the finer side of their being by putting material things to the forefront of their life. So many are oblivious of the soul's need which, in the course of neglect, is being starved of vital ingredients which it needs for sound growth.

Blessed are they who seek to learn the way of the spirit, for unto them shall come an awakening of the higher senses of the mind, which will enable them to see the path they must travel to find what their soul desires. They who are wise shall see the wisdom in what I bring and thus act accordingly.

My joy is in knowing I am helping mankind to learn the greater truths of life that they might soar to the height of spirituality and so experience the bliss of being near to Him, the Creator of all life.

25

THE TEMPLE OF YOUR SOUL

Seek ye the temple of your soul whenever the problems of life seem hard to bear. There you shall find peace and consolation from Him who loves you. The temple of your soul lies within the centre of your being, the powerhouse where God communes. But, if you want to attune with the Divine Spirit of love, then you must learn the art of meditation. They who master this technique shall know how beneficial this can be, for it brings balm to the mind, body and spirit, and thus draws one closer to God, where union can be experienced between you and the Maker of your being.

Each and every child of God holds a spark of the divine light within their soul, which is fanned into a flame from lessons learnt. Thus it is with satisfaction the Father sees the brightness that emanates from those of His children who are learning their lessons well.

To those of you who are seeking the way to spiritual progression, I say to you, be mindful of the fact that you must train your thoughts in a positive way. Thoughts which are negative will only blight your progress. Remember, thoughts are active living things and therefore can perfect or destroy what you want to achieve. Time and time again you could find your strength of will being tested, but they who are strong in mind and spirit shall not be diverted from that which is important to them.

We, who are mentors, experience such joy when we see those in your world, and indeed in ours, seek the light of understanding, for we know they have reached that stage where the soul quickens in anticipation to savour what could be so beneficial to its growth.

We can think of no better way to aid mankind than by bringing truth to bear upon him, for it serves well in releasing those who are bound by ignorance. Regrettably, the passage of time has done little to enlighten man to the full facts of life which could prepare him for the greater life ahead. A vast number of beings arrive in our world confused and often totally unprepared for what awaits them, and so it is with patience and understanding we must guide and support them through the change that has taken place.

I therefore implore those of you who are not in receipt of the literature which could help to prepare you for your entry into that fair land, to seek out what you should know and thus you shall stand enlightened. We, who arc teachers of truth, can only point the way to what could assist you, it is thus up to you whether or not you heed what we have made known to you.

There is, we know, so much to learn about life which we appreciate can be difficult to comprehend in your present state of existence, for you see many conflicting conditions that appear to have no rhyme or reason, which thus perplex you.

Nevertheless, you must endeavour to respect what the Great Father brought into being and try to accept the part He wants you to play in the universal picture of life. And remember, whatever life holds for you, be it bitter or sweet, you can at all times seek the Father in the temple of your soul to thank Him for the good things He sends into your life, and to ask for guidance whenever you are beset by problems that cast shadows your way.

THROUGH THE DOOR OF WISDOM

All must pass through the door of wisdom to learn what truly matters in life, and this in turn helps us to find oneness with God.

The greatness of man comes from his soul development; he who uses the tools of wisdom in his life shall be carving out For himself that which will be delightful to see.

Sadly, so many are held captive by ignorance, which prevents them from Forging ahead to gain what their spirit calls for. We therefore must try to help these unfortunate ones, by breaking the bonds that hold them, with that of enlightenment.

The learning of spiritual truths should be encouraged from an early age, so that they might become well instilled in the growing mind. A strong foundation For soul growth would form from this, thus helping the being to stand firm against life's endurances. What is more, the value of what is learnt would do much towards the making of good, upright citizens who could influence others in the world.

You do well to remember, beloved ones, that every child of God is the weaver of their own destiny. Whatever we do in our life will have a far reaching effect on the way it takes shape. Therefore, it pays to remember this when faced with those things that try the very heart of one's being.

We can never be sure what blessings come in disguise to help us in the shaping of our life. It is so easy to shy away from life's difficulties, but valuable lessons could be lost, and thus are then unable to take part in the forming of that which is important to the graduation of one's spirit. They who turn away from what comes to help them see how to build their life in a constructive way shall Find they are without the essence needed to make it strong.

Be then open to spiritual truths, for they can do much in the way of bringing about a transformation to the pattern of your life, because you would be weaving in threads of the finest kind which are truly touched with gold.

I ask you, dear children of the Great Spirit, to embrace the words I bring, for thus by doing so your soul will gain a goodly measure of what it needs to promote it forward, and remember to allow the light from Him who loves you to be the inspiration behind all that you do.

27

THE TOOLS OF WISDOM

Remember, beloved ones, you are responsible for the way the pattern of your life takes shape, but bear in mind God provides you with the tools of wisdom that you might use them to create one which shows strength and that of beauty from the good you do in life.

The tools of wisdom are many and are God's greatest gift to man, but alas many abuse what He giveth in love and thus the pattern of their life shows a distinctive lack of that which is needed to make it presentable in His sight.

Your world teems with souls who fail to conduct their life in a reasonable way and thus go through life creating difficulties for themselves and others too. It is therefore so pleasing to see those of you who are striving to create a pattern of beauty by your effort and determination to reach perfection. Souls such as you are the back-bone of society because you set a good example for others to follow.

Each and every child of God can follow the path of divine inspiration which teaches one to appreciate the finer side of life, because many truths unfold as one seeks knowledge from the Supreme One. Sadly, a vast number of God's children take the path that spells material gain, giving little or no thought to the riches of a spiritual kind which are lasting and therefore carried with you when the time of transition takes place. All too often we see things of a spiritual nature being swept aside by beings in your world who fail to see the value of them. What treasure they lose by not giving them consideration.

Beloved ones, I trust the truth I bring will light up your life, helping you to see the way in which you can achieve the glories of the spirit. There are those of you, we know, who live in the shadows of doubt, which does nothing to help you progress. We are aware, too, that many of you find life an uphill climb, perhaps because the lessons you are here to learn warrant it, thus to bring greater awareness and strength to your soul, which is necessary for it's growth.

Be then patient with whatever comes to test you and try calmly to accept it in the knowledge that there is a purpose behind all things, which shall be revealed in God's good time to us all one day. Above all, we ask you to hold fast in your mind that the Great Father has provided you with the tools of wisdom to help you shape your life in a positive way. See then that you use them wisely.

SEEK AND YE SHALL FIND

Children of the Great Spirit, I say to you, do not spend your life in the shadows of doubt. Seek and ye shall find that which could help you enter the light of understanding, thus making your pathway easier to tread.

No child of God can expect to make sound progress when marred by ignorance. It prevents one from gaining food for the spirit, which is necessary for its growth. God gives unto His children many opportunities to enable them to light up their lives with those gems called truth, knowledge and wisdom, but alas many spurn them and thus in the mist of uncertainty they must walk, sadly learning the hard way, which regrettably can lead to untold problems for them.

One should never allow oneself to become in a vulnerable situation where one is without knowledge to guide them. This only lowers their soul's capacity to rise to greater heights.

Be rich in the light and the power of the spirit by practising what the Master Jesus taught. This, without doubt, is a sure way of beautifying the pattern of your life, for the threads used from His words hold nothing less than gold. It would be so good if each being of the world tried to centre their life on His teachings. What a vast difference you would see.

Mankind must learn the art of living in a more congenial way, and thus cast out all that is soul-destroying, for the things of a lower nature, such as selfishness and greed, bitterness and hatred are man's greatest enemy, which his spirit can well do without if it is to take on a radiance which is God's dream to see.

Beloved ones, there is not one of you who cannot give something of value to the world to help create more light, which it so sorely needs. Many live in a careless fashion, interested only in their own needs. Where do they think this is going to get them? Not towards reaching those higher levels of consciousness, that is for sure. They simply bar the way to that which is important to spiritual progression.

We try to light the lamp of truth in your lives by the knowledge we bring to help you see the right way to travel, but satisfaction is not always ours to experience when we see our words met with indifference. If one is to tread the path of life successfully, then it is imperative to realise the partaking of spiritual food is a must, for without the nutrients it contains one cannot hope to make first-class progress.

Remember, you are responsible for the way your soul growth takes shape. If you are careless in this respect immaturity will surely show. We build up problems for ourselves when we leave the spiritual aspect of our selves uncared for. It is, after all, the vital part of us and therefore should be given top priority.

29

Prevent lowering the standard of your development by seeking out that which can heighten the level of your soul's education. This is a sure way to God's heart. It pleases Him immensely to see His children rise to the glory of that which He holds in store for them, which, believe me, is well worth striving for.

THE KEY TO HEAVEN

The key to unlock the door to Heaven can be Found by one's diligent search For truth. Truth can show us the way to travel to reach the ever closer to God.

No child of the Great Spirit is without the light of goodness, which can help us see what is needed for sound spiritual growth, but alas many dim this light by their negative thoughts and thus block progress from being made.

You do well to remember,beloved ones, that you can be your own worst enemy by allowing thoughts of negativity to enter your mind. They do nothing to enhance your spirit; on the contrary, they dull the lustre that could be shining there.

The world in which you reside holds numerous beings who live in a fool's paradise, For they truly believe the earth life is the be-all and end-all of existence, thus giving them a reason to behave wholly in a materialistic way, which sadly does nothing to prepare them For the greater life to come, and so they arrive in Spirit World in an ignorant state of mind, knowing not what lies before them. Thus, their education on spiritual matters must begin, if they are to make strides Forward towards gaining that understanding of life's purpose.

The growth of one's soul should be based on truth and knowledge, For without them it cannot function in a positive way. See these gems as stimulants that set growth in motion, which then should be encouraged by ongoing enlightenment. The learning of all that is spiritual never ceases until one reaches the peak of perfection, which of course could take many, many aeons of time.

Life holds much to be discovered and thus we must go on searching for the wisdom that is there to help us advance to those higher dimensions where light, love and power is greater by far than one can imagine. The Great Father wants His children to experience all aspects of life, so that they might qualify for the greatest blessing of all: to dwell with Him in eternal bliss.

Be very sure then, dear children of God, that your aim in life is set on achieving spiritual progression, for you can do no better than this, and thus you shall Find, in your Father's good time, the key to Heaven will be presented to you.

30

THE GIFT OF HEALING

Those whom God has blessed with the gift of healing hold one of the highest forms of mediumship, and thus it should be treasured with care.

Alas, there are amongst the genuine healers of the world those who practise the art of healing for self-gain, which is a low thing to do. God wants to see this work carried out in love and compassion with a true desire to help those in need utmost in the mind. The Father God is not fooled. He sees clearly into our hearts and minds, nothing is hidden From Him.

The healing ones must at all times remember they have been given a privileged role to play and therefore should ensure their conduct is one that does not invite criticism in any way. Indeed, all work carried out for God must be done with the right attitude of mind. If it is not, then we fail in our duty to Him.

We know From experience and therefore understand that tasks of a spiritual nature can be hard at times, but if you persevere with what you do in a light-hearted way, knowing you are being of service, immense satisfaction will be yours to experience. God brings joy to those who serve Him.

The healing work can be very rewarding in more ways than one, and thus it is always enriched with the light of the Christ Spirit, because it is something dear to His heart. He understands so well the plight of the sick and suffering ones, and is ever trying to bring peace and comfort to them.

One of the sad facts of life is that your world holds so many beings who suffer a drug or alcohol addiction, which not only affects their body, but the mind, too. Such ones have an inborn weakness and therefore are easily drawn into these things of corruption. The result this has on their soul is truly a pathetic one.

The healing ministering ones from Spirit side of life indeed take on a difficult task in trying to help them break Free From their craving. The resistance they put up is by no means easy to break down. However, we can be sure these good souls never waver in the course of their work, no matter how laborious it might be.

To those of you who are working in a healing capacity, I say to you blend God's power which flows through you with all the love you can muster. Love is a most potent thing, which if used correctly can conquer a myriad of ills.

We know this path of service you take is a responsible one, but if you work at all times within the light of God, letting love and compassion rule what you do, then you can rest assured that what you carry out will be blessed by the Great Spirit.

There are those who tend to hide their healing gift because they feel inadequate about using it. Such thoughts of negativity need to be overcome by using the key to positive thinking, or that which God has blessed them with will fail to be used to aid others. This is a sad thing to see when there are numerous sick ones needing help.

Beloved ones, never forget to appreciate the value of those gifts which Him Host High sees fit to grant unto you. He wants you to handle them with care for the sole purpose of bringing good into the lives of others.

May my words open up new avenues of thought for you to ponder upon, to thus help you in whatever service you perform. Be ever true to your Maker and you will find His hand shall guide you in all you undertake to do.

THE WONDER OF CREATION

How many of you truly appreciate the wonder of Creation which God's almighty hand fashioned so well? Sadly, there are those of His children who abuse what He has made, in a most insensitive way. It is difficult to comprehend when one knows a spark of the Divine One lies within them. Souls such as these allow the destructive force of life to enter their being which tries to corrupt the marvels of God's Kingdom by its very nature to gain power over Him. But God's strength of will would never allow this lower force to dominate and thus destroy what He achieved.

The world the Great Father brought into being holds many wonderful things which show clearly the intelligence of His great mind. We, from the higher realms, see with clarity the wisdom He displayed when putting into operation that which His creative mind laboured upon. I therefore ask you to show respect for the Father's Creation, and thus let it be seen that you are supporting what He worked hard to contrive.

Blessed are they who serve Him and who pledge to be faithful and true in whatever work they are inspired to do, for they shall share the secrets of His heart, thus enabling them to see how very wise and purposeful His miraculous mind can be.

We know the Father's Creation can appear to be a somewhat complicated affair to those who are not enlightened beings. Many are perplexed by some of the happenings which take place and which do not seem in keeping with a God of love. But, I say to you, do not judge Him by what you see, for you have not yet seen the whole picture of life and therefore are not in a position to know what is truly right or wrong. You do well to remember many of the dire things of life are brought about by man's ignorance and lack of insight, which should be helping him to see how wrong it is to break the laws of life with acts that go against His grain.

Beloved ones, I ask you to view more closely the wonderful things of Creation and thus you would see and appreciate more fully the greatness of your Father God Who has given us so much to use and enjoy to help us in our learning.

HANDS THAT HEAL

I say unto those who are blessed with the gift of healing, you hold one of the greatest gifts of all and you are without doubt close to the Master's heart, for you are seen as His valuable workers.

Be then never forgetful of the trust He places in you. Allow no thought of using this gift for self gain to enter your mind. Remember, you are being used to help the sick and suffering ones of the world in service to God. To abuse this by feathering your own nest for services rendered is wrong, unless there should be some good justifiable reason that warrants this.

Hands that heal can do much to help bring calmness to a troubled mind. Beings who are afflicted by mental illness can often experience the most distressing symptoms which are hard to bear. Souls such as these need special understanding, and most certainly a listening ear. The need to unburden themselves is essential to thus allow the release of those jumbled thoughts that so confuse their minds.

We in Spirit are so very aware of the healing help needed in your world, and God is ever seeking suitable channels to use for this rewarding work. But, alas, it is not easy to find worthy souls, whom He needs to be dedicated, and who show a loving, compassionate heart. Sadly, your world is found rather wanting in this respect.

Physical pain and suffering is the scourge of man's life, for it can deny him the right to enjoy the things that could be important to him. But that which is endured could be helped by the power of the healing rays, which come from the heart of God, to thus flow through those hands that heal. No problem should be seen as hopeless, for one never knows what might transpire when seeking help from a spiritual source.

The Great Master works incessantly to bring upliftment to mankind, and you can be sure wherever healing takes place the light from Spirit shines there.

Blessed indeed are they who serve in a healing capacity, for they shall merit that which will beautify their soul.

Many of God's children, we know, are sceptical of spiritual healing, and are inclined to dismiss it before giving it a fair trial. Thus their ignorance of such matters could deter them from proving what can be gained and of the value which is derived from it.

They who scorn the precious things of the spirit may well find the need to embrace them some day, for one can never tell what lies ahead of us. Wise is the man who keeps an open mind on all things, for it allows the seeds of truth to enter therein, where they can be used to bring a higher degree of understanding, whereas they would not otherwise have been given the opportunity to leave their mark on his mind.

The pearls of God's heart are undoubtedly those beloved ones who work tirelessly for the good of humanity. Thus we see their spirits enveloped in the hues which represent their work, and this is indeed a lovely sight to see.

There is not one of you who is not capable of giving service to God in some shape or form. The work of the spirit is endless, and we gladly welcome those who offer their services. It matters not whether your choice be great or small, all help is most gratefully received, and I would have you know, dear children of the Great Spirit, as you give of yourself, we are so very aware of the sweetness that emanates from your flowering soul.

DIM NOT YOUR LIGHT

Beloved ones, we all have a spark of the divine light within us and thus we should take care not to dim this by adopting a careless attitude towards life, which only lowers one's soul to a level of consciousness that offers nothing but ruin. Far better to kindle the spark of light into a flame by living your lives responsibly, creating good where you can.

There is not one of you who is not given opportunities to radiate the light of the Great Spirit. Sadly, your world teems with souls who choose to ignore them, basically because their lives are too bound up with the material, leaving little or no time for things of a spiritual nature which, if they only realised, should be their main concern.

It is not hard to see the lack of spirituality on your earth planet. Plainly, it is so visible in all we view. If only mankind would learn to conduct his life in a sensible way and try to cultivate respect for his fellow-beings, a far different picture would be seen. If there is no pulling together in the things that matter, how can you expect your world to change for the better. There is too much negativity around. More positivity is needed to make for better relationships. What a transformation there would be if all God's children practised the art of sharing and caring, with love showing prominently in what they carry out.

The foundation of your lives should be made strong by using the tools of knowledge and wisdom. By failing to take the trouble to do this, soul progress cannot successfully be made.

The seeds of truth I try to sow into your minds I trust will grow to therefore enable you to advance spiritually-wise. My work for God primarily involves teaching the important factors of life, which one cannot afford to be without if we are to climb the stairway of life to reach the highest point of spirituality where the Great One rules supreme.

Be ever conscious of the fact, beloved ones, that you are responsible for the way your life takes shape. The very essence of your thoughts and deeds must be of the purest kind. If they are not, your soul will suffer the consequences and thus be devoid of beauty.

THE LAWS OF LIFE

So many inhabitants in your world show no respect for the laws of life, which should be in keeping with all you do. Nothing can ever be gained by opposing that which the Great Father expects you to honour in His Name. All too often man allows his lower self to dominate, thus bringing to the fore behavioural problems which can be soul destroying and which can prevent him from ascending the ladder of life to reach spiritual maturity.

Man's life on earth should be seen as one where he can gain soul promotion by accepting the challenges God sets before him. They who are wise will accept them gladly, knowing they can quicken one's progress.

If one is to truly learn the way of the spirit, then knowledge must be sought, and thus reasoned with, for one should only accept that which they feel comfortable with. The wise ones of the Spirit are ever conscious of the enlightenment needed in your world, and therefore wait to guide those who seek their help. These humble and dedicated souls who project such love in their desire to aid mankind are indeed beings of the light who dwell in the power of God.

Be then sincere in your search for truth and you shall find their guidance forthcoming. Man has much to learn about God's Plan for us all, which often he finds a mystery to him because the level of his understanding, has not yet reached its peak, but as he advances towards the light of realisation, he shall indeed see with clarity how every part of life's jigsaw fits into place perfectly. God provides many lovely things for man to enjoy, but all too often they are taken for granted or abused by his insensitive attitude to life, which in his foolishness he fails to respect.

If man is to evolve in a positive way, then he must learn to play the game of life by learning the right way to live. He must put into practice the laws of life and abide by their worth, because spiritual progress stems from their validity.

Time and time again, we see beings in your world turn away from the path of righteousness through the influence of others who do not believe in God. Regrettably, we are often helpless in our attempt to guide them away from the narrow-mindedness of those who refuse to see beyond their own beliefs, because we must at all times respect their freewill.

There does, however, appear to be much controversy in your world relating to spiritual matters, which can create confusion in man's mind. But if he would only search for the answers to that which perplexes him, he would find what he needs to enlighten his mind.

We, who serve the Great Spirit, know without a shadow of doubt that He is the priceless jewel in the centre of the universe, whose power is great indeed. Without Him, we are nothing. Be then respectful of all He stands for. What is more, help Him to keep order in the world by obeying the laws of life, thus you shall know you are playing your part in His scheme of things and proving too that you are a true child of Him, the Creator of your being.

THE GIFT OF MEDIUMSHIP

To those of God's children who have been blessed with the gift of mediumship, I say to you, remember you are entrusted with this in His name, therefore be careful not to abuse it by allowing your little ego to dominate or you will degrade what you have been privileged to do.

Mediumship should be practised in all sincerity, with thoughtfulness given to all who seek your help. Bear in mind you carry the torch of truth to show others the way, be then trustworthy when guiding them.

Those of you who serve God hold a grave responsibility not to be taken lightly. The key to success lies in your ability to exercise control over the tasks you are inspired to do. A will-o-the wisp attitude will not do. Dedication, reliability and steadfastness must rank high in all work carried out for God. Those who work in a half-hearted fashion are not worthy of His trust and therefore could not be considered for greater missions allocated to those who show themselves to be strong in mind and spirit.

Mediumship carried out in the truest sense of the word can do so much to help humanity, bringing comfort and joy, and hope from enlightenment, into the lives of many. But alas there are those who use their gift for self gain, thus corrupting that which God has bestowed upon them. Mediums such as these cannot possibility attract guides who are virtuous, because they would not be able to attune to their wavelength. They are more likely to draw those from the lower regions of Spirit World who are limited in what they can bring, be it power, knowledge or enlightenment. Thus their standard of mediumship would be one of low order.

But to those who are loyal and prove to be true servants to God, I tell you this. The light of the Master shines forth upon them. This gentle soul is ever in the midst of life, guiding the footsteps of souls who serve in the Father's Name. He walks closely with those who carry true love in their heart.

Mediumship based on love will indeed surely prosper, for it holds the essence of God. Love is the key that can open the door to the treasure of the spirit which could help to promote your work. Mediumship can be so rewarding if used in a constructive way, for you can create a wealth of good in the world by allowing your guides to channel through you knowledge of a meaningful kind which could help many souls to reach the light of understanding, which is oft-times difficult to find in your world which holds so much ignorance.

Be then protective of your gift. Allow nothing to taint it. Rightly used, it can dispel fear which often plagues many who have no knowledge of life after death. So honour what the One Most High has blessed you with, for does He not give you a privileged role to play in the great universal picture of life.

36

ALL CREATURES GREAT AND SMALL

Beloved ones, it is with deep concern I feel the need to speak on the way in which an increasing number of God's dumb creatures are being exploited in your world by ruthless ones who oft-times treat them in a most deplorable way. It is hard to believe they are children of the Great Spirit. Mankind would do well to remember their lower brethren are a part of God's Plan and therefore should be respected and cared for in a rightful manner. They who inflict misery, pain and suffering upon them shall indeed find they have much to answer for.

All creatures both great and small must be allowed to live out their allotted life span in a natural way. Fear, loss of freedom and cruelty imposed upon them can bruise the soul within which in many cases takes some time to heal. I therefore advise man most strongly to think before he takes it upon himself to carry out acts on God's dumb and helpless creatures without some justifiable cause.

Your world shares a great responsibility where God places in man's trust the care of His lower creation. Therefore, man must see that justice is carried out when they are seen to be under threat. The seeds of loving kindness are not always given space in man's heart where they could grow and find expression in helping to bring out the best in him. Sadly, the nature of man is such that he is inclined to overlook the important things of life essential to his growth. He could so enrich his soul by striving to do good in the world.

Opportunity awaits all who desire to undertake work for God, so why not be a bearer of truth to help free those trapped by ignorance. Carriers of knowledge, too, are needed to enlighten the minds of many. All tasks for God are appreciated and thus earn one the joy of promotion. We who are messengers of the Great Spirit carry with us truth and wisdom which we gladly impart to all who want to increase their spiritual values to advance further into the light of God.

Alas, there are many of His children who shows signs of decay in their way of thinking by the very fact that they are allowing the lower things of life to dominate them. One day they shall see with eyes of the spirit and then realise how foolish they have been, for material things are of no avail when one enters that fair land. All you carry with you is your character and what you have earnt in a spiritual way which determines your next stage of existence.

Be then wise, dear children of the Great Spirit, and try to live your life in a good and upright way. Be faithful and true to Him who loves you. Furthermore, be kind and considerate to the Father's lower creation who are vulnerable to man's domination over them. Bear in mind they are evolving too like you and therefore need your love, help and understanding.

LIGHT UP YOUR LIFE

Do not flounder in the darkness of ignorance. Light up your life with knowledge of eternal truth which is so necessary if your soul is to quicken its progress to thus reach that level of consciousness where it becomes more aware of the presence of God.

Knowledge born of eternal truth likens to an anchor in one's life, for it provides a form of stability which prevents us from sinking to the depths of despair when the tests of life appear to be intolerable. The material world, however, with all its problems, is not without advantages, because the experiences one encounters open up our awareness to the truth of life, which must be faced if we are to develop that understanding of what lies behind God's great Plan.

God wants His children to learn what is important to the world at large, so that His dream for us might materialise in the way He intended. Thus, we must try to help Him bring this ideal to fruition by seeking the knowledge that enables us to see the way in which we can aid Him.

Many of you, we know, work for the Great Spirit in a wholehearted way, unselfishly giving of your time to carry out tasks for Him, and this is so good to see. Souls such as you bring light to the world which is greatly needed, for much darkness is being created by many who allow that evil twosome selfishness and greed to dominate their lives.

Sadness overwhelms us as we view the picture of your world. We see mistakes being made by numerous souls who foolishly choose to ignore the tools of wisdom God provides to help His children build conditions of solidity to thus enable peace, harmony and goodwill to prevail.

They who act in an irresponsible manner would do well to bear in mind that they will gain nothing but misery. No one escapes the wrong they do, the price must be paid. This is the law of life. Time and time again we from Spirit World speak of the need for unity in your world where true love and understanding might blossom from Man's heart, thus eliminating the aggression that rules today, but alas all too often our words fail to make an impact on Man's mind, and so he continues in the same old way creating problems which could be avoided if only he would heed those words of truth.

Your earth plane holds much for mankind, but sadly it is being slowly, but surely, destroyed by Man's careless and reckless behaviour. He must give it the respect it deserves or find himself facing a very sorry state of affairs which will leave him sorely troubled. Wise is he who travels the path of righteousness, better by far than finding himself on the road of destruction because he refuses to listen to reason.

Beloved ones, light up your life with the wisdom I bring and thus you can be sure you are being guided in the right direction. Be kind, be gentle to all living things. Value God's Creation, remember much love and thought has gone into it and may I remind you, lest you forget, that you are a part of it.

LAY UP YOUR TREASURE IN HEAVEN

How many of your are laying up treasure in Heaven from acts of kindness and by serving God and your fellow-men? Far too many of God's children travel through life gathering treasure of an earthly kind which holds no true and lasting value, and therefore is useless to them when the time of transition takes place.

Much wiser to gain the treasure of the spirit which is blessed by God and thus will serve you well in the greater life to come. We, who have reached a higher level of consciousness know without doubt the only way to true contentment is by placing spiritual values to the forefront of your life, because they will always stand you in good stead.

God is a wise and loving Father who is only too well aware of His children's needs and desires,which you can be sure receive consideration. But, one must remember, because we are born of Him, He and He alone knows what is best for us, and so we must accept what He sends into our life and thus bear in mind the lesson it holds for us to learn.

Beloved ones, no better way could you find to God's heart than by bringing light into another's life, or by creating love and peace wherever you go, for the Great Father emanates these things and thus wants His children to do the same. So much needs to be done in your world to bring about wholesome conditions essential to man's growth, which is often stunted by the curse of ignorance which has plagued him for so long.

The Aquarian Age, however, shall bring a stirring to man's heart and many will hunger for knowledge as never before. Slowly but surely man's attitude to the material things of life shall change, thus seeing them as valueless against the prizes of the spirit. We see the advancing years heralding in new methods of teaching which shall stimulate the mind. The young will particularly find them easier to comprehend, for oft-times they discover the old doctrines difficult to understand, which does nothing to evoke an interest in them.

One's character can be so enriched by the correct method of teaching, for it can touch the innermost feelings of the soul. Do not doubt the changes the New Age will surely bring, for a cleansing process must take place to clear that which has tainted the world for so long.

May peace reign in your hearts, beloved ones. Remember to be kind in word and deed and forget not to lay up your treasure in Heaven by living the good way of life, for this will benefit you greatly one day.

LET NOT YOUR HEART BE TROUBLED

Such simple words, we know, but not easy to abide by when the problems of life are hard to bear. I therefore bring you the light of understanding that you might find solace in knowing that all you endure is for the good of the soul.

We, who were once resident in your world, know only too well of the difficulties earth life can bring, and thus say to you, should they rest heavily upon you try to accept them with good grace, knowing they are but a means to test your spirit.

Alas, a great number of you allow the intricate things of life to cast shadows around you, therefore preventing the light of reason to shine through, and so your life could appear to be an uphill struggle because you are unable to see the truth which lies behind the things which come to test the very heart of your being.

How many of you are truly aware of the God-force within you that can help you brave the storms of life, which oft-times leave one in a state of confusion which disrupts the peace of one's mind. I therefore suggest you learn to value the power that can so uplift you in the complex times of your life, and appreciate too the strength you gain from it.

Your world teems with souls who have no idea how their progress could be helped by attunement with the Infinite One whose watchful eye is aware of our needs. He places before us the means to draw on His help by the simple method of meditation, which all can learn the art of.

We, from the higher planes of Spirit World, are constantly trying to infuse your world with our knowledge gained through aeons of time, but sadly we often find the mind of man is not always receptive to what is transmitted to him, and so it is with regret we see our words failing to imprint upon his mind that which could help his soul ascend to a higher level of consciousness where it could move into the light of greater knowledge.

Alas, time and time again, man can be his own worst enemy by creating stumbling blocks from the careless way he lives. He therefore must endeavour to use wisdom in his life and thus he would find it enables him to see how to avoid those things that are brought about by his own thoughtless making.

To those of you who feel you are battling against all odds to rise above the obstacles that beset you, I say to you, let not your heart be troubled, neither let it be afraid, for God helps those who help themselves and thus, with His ministering ones, He will guide you through the testing times of your life.

THE SEEDS OF TRUTH

Beloved ones, by the grace of God, I come to enlighten your pathway. This is not an easy task I undertake to do because many of God's children do not wish to learn spiritual truths. Happy to live in a state of materialism, they close their minds to that which is crucial to the development of their souls. But, difficult as my task might be, I must endeavour to open the minds of those who are biased against such things, to plant the seeds of truth therein.

There are many in your world who suffer through the ignorance of others. War, famine, sickness and disease have left their mark on innocent victims of such things. These unfortunate ones often have to struggle through the darkness of despair to reach the light of understanding. It is truly a pitiful sight to see.

They who are responsible for the plight such souls are in must one day face retribution because no one has the right to bring the undesirable things of life unto another.

Many beings in your world are engaged in activities that hold no scope for the fine things of life, thus the spiritual aspect of their being is sadly neglected. The Great Father wants to see His children trying to gain a high standard of spirituality to help them advance towards the greater glories of His Kingdom, which you can be sure are wonderful to see.

Beloved ones, try to see your life as one of purpose, knowing the lessons you are here to learn are to awaken the higher senses of your mind where you might see things in true perspective. Try not to sour the sweetness of life with acts of treason. Be true to yourself and to your fellow beings who too must learn the wisdom of life.

I beseech thee to place value on the words I speak because they could help you progress. And in truth I say to you, they who walk the way of the Lord shall not hunger for the food of the spirit, for the good Master takes care of all who enter His fold.

This radiant being never fails to impress us in Spirit World by the knowledge He brings, gained by His endeavour to reach oneness with God. We, who have seen the learned Master in the light of truth, stand enthralled by the power He brings and thus we feel humble in His sight.

I, who am a mentor, tell you this, no soul enters the door of divinity without earning the right to do so. One therefore must go through numerous learning stages until awareness and complete understanding of life and its purpose has been gained. But this process could take many lifetimes, and so it is with patience and perseverance one's soul must endeavour to strive, learning from the lessons life holds, until at last it is ready to enter the door to the Power of all life where it merits the right to meet with the Supreme Spirit of

Love. Thus, the soul stands in the light of all it has achieved, pure in mind and spirit, worthy to be with the Creator.

May the seeds of truth I bring blossom in your soul, helping you to gain the privilege of union with Him who gave you life.

THE PATH TO GOD

The path to the source of all life is alas one less travelled because so many of God's children are without knowledge to help them see what great opportunity it holds, where their soul can mature from that which is learnt in a more profound way.

Time and time again, we from higher planes of Spirit World endeavour to help mankind see what could be fruitful to his spirit, but all too often the words we try to channel through man's mind are rejected by the very fact that he places before all else things material. We cannot emphasise too strongly the importance that should be given to soul development. Progress to higher levels of consciousness stems from this, and thus allows one to attune with beings who hold knowledge which can inspire you to move steadily up the stairway of life.

Many of you, we know, are ever seeking to gain greater wisdom, which is a joy to see. Souls such as you have indeed seen the light of understanding, which has drawn you towards that which truly matters in life, thus your footsteps shall be guided to reach the power governing all of life, for you, beloved ones, have chosen the path to God.

To those who are without the truth of the spirit, I say to you, they who earnestly seek enlightenment shall not search in vain, for there are teachers dwelling in the light of God who await to teach souls who show they are ready and willing to walk the path of deeper meaning.

Not one child of the Great Father need ever feel they are not given the opportunity to spiritual progression, for the Father sends into all His children's lives challenges which, if accepted in the right attitude of mind, can do so much to promote one's soul growth.

The pattern of your life could be very much enhanced by the weaving in of those threads that come from a spiritual source. They who use the threads of the spirit can be sure their life's pattern will be one showing beauty.

Waste not your time, beloved ones, in pursuing only that which is materialistic, thinking this will bring contentment to your life. True satisfaction comes from that which fulfils the needs of your soul. Wise beings will bear this in mind, and thus make sure it is served well with the good things of the spirit.

Doubt not the words I speak, for they come on wings of love from a dimension that sends forth light from the Christ Spirit.

CAST NO SHADOWS

Children of the Great Spirit, avoid casting shadows in your lives by negative thinking, or you will prevent the light of your spirit from shining through. Your life could be one of brightness and joy by learning the code of the spirit which holds the key to enlightenment.

Sadly, so few show a keen interest in searching for the truth of life which makes for positive thinking, enabling one's soul to progress with confidence towards the Kingdom of God. There are, we know, a goodly number of beings on the earth plane who are trapped by ignorance. Their way of living brings them nothing but discontent. True peace and harmony cannot come to those who are without the key to knowledge.

Knowledge helps our soul to advance to those higher dimensions where it can gain satisfaction from the wisdom that lies there. They who remain in a state of ignorance lose out on so much. But, God the Father has blessed them with freewill, and this must be respected, in spite of the fact that we long to help them move forward into the light of all that spells progress.

Enlightened souls are able to face the trials and tribulations of life without trepidation. They see them for what they are, and so try to drum up courage and goodwill to overcome them, knowing they are but tests for the spirit.

Those who allow themselves to be daunted by the snags of life cannot hope to achieve soul promotion; their strength of character would be found wanting, and therefore will need to be worked on if progress is to be made.

Beloved ones, bear in mind you all have the ability to evolve in a positive way, but you must try not to create shadows in your lives by lack of insight which, sad to say, is behind the many problems your world is holding today. The power of the spirit is always there to help you rise above the lower things of life. However, you must learn how to attune to this with the right attitude of mind. Half-hearted attempts will only prove unsatisfactory.

Be true to yourselves, listen to your spirit, and thus be guided by what it calls for.

Few take the time or the trouble to do so. They much prefer to listen to the voice of materialism which promises to satisfy the cravings of the lower self, which alas is seen as more important. But we, who have advanced spiritually, know this can only be a temporary affair that cannot continue when they enter the Greater World.

They who wisely invest in the spiritual shall, without doubt, find they have laid a strong foundation for good progress. But they who fail to do this will start their new life poor indeed. Thus, the task of gaining access

43

to the Summer land, the realm of beauty and delight, will prove to be hard. No one can enter therein until they earn the right to do so. This will not be easy for those who have placed material gain before all else.

Dear children of God, take note of what I say. My privilege is to guide you, helping you to cast out those doubts and fears which can plague one when in a state of ignorance. Be happy in the knowledge that much awaits those who strive to learn what is on the other side of the coin of life. It thus rests with each one of you to make the effort to accomplish this.

TRUST IN THE LORD

Beloved ones, be content to put your trust in the Lord, knowing His code of conduct is one you can follow to show you the way to the Father of all. One need never doubt the wisdom and integrity of this fine soul Who brought His teachings to bear upon the world that man might learn to understand what should be important to him.

Blessed are they who practice what He taught, for they shall emanate the golden ray of spirituality which can touch others by the power it brings. They who live in the light of the Lord shall not fear that which comes to test their spirit, for they know their strength will uphold them in whatever tries to cast them down.

How many of you are aware of how the pattern of your life could be greatly enriched by the careful blending of those things which can make you strong in mind and spirit? Alas, a great number of the inhabitants in your world have no idea how important it is to blend spiritual values into their lives, and thus they fail to create what God wants them to do.

Sadly, your world weighs heavily in ignorance, which stems from man's lack of enlightenment, and this creates problems for him. But this can be rectified by seeking the light of understanding where he could gain insight into that which would help him become aware of his soul's need.

I would have you know, beloved ones, the good Master continues to work incessantly for the benefit of mankind, which I can assure you is not an easy task because of the many conflicting conditions in your world which have created a mist of uncertainty around numerous souls who are finding it difficult to find a harmonious way of life.

Dear children of the Great Spirit, so much could you gain by gathering unto yourself the teachings of the Lord, for His wealth of knowledge can be used for the betterment of your life to thus help you grow in spiritual splendour.

Trust then, beloved ones, trust in the Lord and be content in knowing His wisdom shall guide you if you would but believe in the greatness of His worth.

THE PATH LESS TRAVELLED

The turmoil manifesting in your world clearly shows the path of spirituality is one less travelled. Alas, the majority of mankind far from hold the values they should, and respect in the truest meaning of the word is rarely seen today.

The spiritual aspect of Man's being is often starved of those vital nutrients it needs for sound growth. This is because Man allows his lower self to dominate to such an extent that little or no thought is given to the welfare of the higher self. One day he will experience feelings of deep regret when he at last realises how unwise he has been in letting the material hold sway over the spiritual.

We know from experience that your world holds many temptations which can lure one away from the path or righteousness, but they who truly desire to advance towards the Supreme One will stand firm against the forces which try to tempt them to change direction.

Time and time again throughout your lives you could be faced with situations that look to bear the Name of God, but, unless you are sure they hold that element of goodness, allow them not to influence your lives.

Man has much to learn and therefore his main aim in life should be in gaining truth, knowledge, and wisdom. They are the most valuable of things one could ever possess. Once acquired, they are yours for all time and thus will serve you well. Pity those who turn away from spiritual literature, for they miss out on so much that could help to prepare them for the greater life to come.

We mentors from Spirit World are constantly trying to feed Man's mind with truth, but this is truly not an easy task, for so many refuse to accept what we bring. Again and again, we try various methods to thus enlighten Man, but alas success is not always our joy to receive in such matters.

Beloved ones, do not allow idleness to feature in your lives. There is much one can do to help make your world a better place to live in. Search around and you will surely find a task to do which could prove to be of value.

The path of spirituality would not be less travelled if mankind took the trouble to seek knowledge which could help them to see the opportunities which lie there. But, alas, it appears so few want to learn the way to progression, because they are foolishly content to strive for material gain, thinking this is all that matters. What treasure they lose by not striving instead for spiritual things which could so enhance their spirit.

FOOD FOR THOUGHT

Beloved ones, may the words I bring give you food for thought, thus helping you to see things perhaps from another angle to which you might not be accustomed.

Man in his present state cannot fully appreciate the working of God's great mind. Many things in life are often perplexing to him, mainly because his level of consciousness prevents him from gaining access to the truth of that which he finds difficult to comprehend. But, man need not be restricted in knowledge. Opportunities for him to graduate to higher levels of learning are there for him to grasp, but alas more often than not he turns away from them, and thus in ignorance he remains.

It is a sad fact of life that so few seek spiritual education which they need to enable them to evolve in the way they should. Man can be foolish in the way he lives his life; often he fails to get his priorities right and therefore is inclined to put the material on a pedestal where it is allowed to dominate him in a useless fashion, which gets him nowhere but on the path of ruin where his soul suffers the consequence of neglect.

Be wise, dear children of the Great Spirit, and tend your soul with care, for its growth depends on the way you live. Should your life be one holding spiritual values, then you can rest assured you are moving in the right direction where the light of God shines forth upon you. But, if you are living in such a way that you are wrapped up in materialism, then your soul is being deprived of reaching maturity, for it cannot possibly accomplish this goal if you fail to encourage it to do so.

To those of you who are starting out on the path of spiritual progression, I say to you, be not discouraged by any setbacks you might experience; look upon them as tests to try your spirit. Strive on with courage in your heart, for there is much to be gained by pursuing this path of deeper meaning.

We look at the state of your world and thus realise how few there are who are spiritually motivated. So many of mankind are dragging themselves deeper and deeper into the mire by their senseless behaviour. which is serving no purpose. If they could only see the darkness they are creating by their irresponsibility, a change in their attitude might come about for the picture of their lifestyle is not a pleasant one to see. In fact, it would show them they are heading for destruction.

Let that word called wisdom guide you in all you do. Encourage the light of goodness to come into your lives by carrying out acts of kindness and by showing others the way to the path of righteousness. Thus, by doing so, you are helping your own spiritual unfoldment to blossom forth where its beauty sends the perfume of its flowering to your Father God.

FLOW WITH THE TIDE OF LIFE

They who flow with the tide of life are moving in harmony with God and therefore progress for them shall be a most rewarding affair.

It is imperative, beloved ones, that those of you who are not fully aware of what life is about seek first the rudiments of this before trying to reach out for knowledge you are not yet ready for. All knowledge must come in stages, for the mind to truly grasp it as it should. It is not wise to try and walk before you can crawl, so to speak, because impatience tells you so. This is a sure way of missing out on that which is important to good progression.

Life has so much to offer mankind to enable him to reach that level of consciousness which helps his soul to soar forth towards the Godhead. Sadly, your world shows all too clearly how Man abuses those things God grants for his advancement.

The Kingdom of the Lord awaits all who earn the right to enter therein. This means, amongst other things, allowing your higher self that freedom to dominate. It must not be blocked by the demands of the lower aspect of your being, which can offer no fulfilment or peace of mind, nor can it bring you the glories of the greater world, because it does not have that thread of gold running through it linking you to that higher force which gives your soul access to such things.

Remember, at all times, the gems you should be seeking are those holding the value of the spirit. If you are rich in these, your spiritual crown shall be indeed a fine one to see. No child of God need be swept along by a current of uncertainty because ignorance be the bane of their life. Knowledge awaits all who take the time out to seek it. They who foolishly do not bother cannot expect to flow with the tide of life, for they have not gained what it needs to do this.

Great is the power and the love of God, and thus we should put our trust in Him and believe He has our best interest at heart, in spite of what we see happening in the world, which creates doubt in the mind.

Mankind, however, must learn to realise that the chaos prevailing has been brought about by wrong-doing, which simply means Man is not playing the game of life fairly. Therefore, he cannot expect to see anything else but disruption taking place. He must try to get his act together, and thus to be true to his Maker, instead of blaming Him when things go wrong. They who are creating difficulties in the world are working against their heavenly Father, which is so wrong, and thus will gain them nothing in the way of respect from Him.

Be wise in what you do by thinking in terms of your soul's development. You can so easily mar this by being careless in thought, word and deed. Invite the light of God into your lives by working for Him, thus by doing so your passage to higher dimensions will be ensured.

BEAR YOUR CROSS WITH GOODWILL

To those of you who are carrying a burden in some shape or form, I say to you bear it with goodwill, for God the Father would not have placed it with you without some good reason. It is wise to allow the power of your resistance to lay low in such matters, because by opposing that which is yours to carry will not be to your credit.

One can learn much from situations calling for strength of character. This is not always easy, we know, but one's soul gains good growth in the process, which enables it to progress forward. It is not wise to lose sight of the fact that God wants us, His children, to experience all aspects of life, some of which might not be to our liking. But, we cannot shy away from reality, it is all a part of our education which we must accept if our soul is to graduate.

Life holds many tests in one way or another, and although we may find them wearisome, one should try to accept them with good grace in the knowledge that they are but stepping stones to help us to reach the many wonderful things God has in store for us, just waiting to be embraced.

We understand that life for many of you seems to be one long hard climb where little joy seems to be forthcoming but, beloved ones, take comfort in knowing that from the lesson you are learning, tough as it might be, will come much good, giving radiance to your spirit. There are numerous beings who try to side-track those things in life which call for sacrifice. This, of course, is their prerogative, but they cannot expect to show sound soul development.

Sadly, it is a fact that your world shows little humanitarianism. It seems a large majority of souls are only interested in their own welfare. Indeed, they have much to learn. The Great Spirit wants to see His children helping each other in a way He would approve of. Sharing and caring should not be done in a half-hearted fashion, this will not bring blessings from God.

So much time is wasted in the lives of many by carrying out fruitless things of no value. This is sad to see when there are numerous tasks they could take on to assist others. Those of you who are the carers of the world are indeed seen in a light shedding golden rays. This is truly lovely to see from my side of life. We only wish many more souls would show the splendour of this by doing things that are worthwhile.

Beloved ones, your earth life is so short in comparison with life in Spirit, and not one of you knows when the Great Father will call you back home to that fair land. So, in the course of your daily lives, why not try to sow seeds of goodness that they might grow and flourish for others to remember you by.

THE SOURCE OF ALL LIFE

Beloved ones, turn to Him, the source of all life, when guidance is needed in your lives, For He and He alone knows what is truly right For you. In quietude, attune to Him and you will Find peace entering your soul, uplifting your spirit in a way that shall leave you in no doubt of His Presence with you.

Alas, so many tend to overlook the fact that God is the source of all life from whence their spirit cometh. We from the higher planes of life are anxious that you do not forget, in the course of your busy lives, the creative force behind all things. Time and time again, we see the Father's work of art being abused by those who lack sensitivity. Destruction of the wonders of the world is a dreadful thing to see and they who have a hand in this shall not escape retribution. One day they will have no choice but to judge themselves harshly, which can be a soul-racking thing.

Man has much to learn. He should not run away with the idea that life is a game he can play to suit his own ends. It does not work that way. If he chooses to act irresponsibly, then a penalty will have to be paid.

Discipline in your world is indeed sadly lacking, which clearly shows why things are out of control. All in all, your planet tells a sorry tale. The lower self of a great many is being allowed to come to the fore, hence the reason for the dire happenings you see today.

Thankfully, there are a goodly number or fine souls who are trying to bring better conditions into being, but this is not an easy task when others fail to co-operate. However, we in Spirit stand confident in the knowledge that good will always rule over evil. God's power is strong, indeed a force to be reckoned with, and therefore He will never allow that of a lower nature to take hold to reign supreme.

The children of God have much to learn about Him. He is not some fantasy conjured up in one's mind. He is a Spirit of great power, love, knowledge, and wisdom, Who created the universe in all its splendour for His children to enjoy and to learn from. He is the source of all life behind all creation. Let us not Forget this, come what may.

He must not be blamed for the disasters of the world. Man has created these in his ignorance. Mankind, however, must not use this as an excuse to cover up his behaviour. Knowledge awaits him in plenty: he must find time to seek it. You all have the ability to learn the wisdom of life which makes for better living.

I come in love to point the way that you might travel in the right direction. Thank your Father God for the blessings He sends into your lives, instead or taking them for granted, which so many of you do. Above all, strive to do good in the world to thus bring better conditions into being so that peace and harmony might at long last prevail.

49

THE SEEDS OF GOODNESS

Far too many, by their selfish lifestyle, are not planting seeds of goodness to thus allow beauty to emanate from their soul. The seeds they are planting are of such poor quality that nothing but ugliness can come out of them, which not only darkens their spirit, but casts gloom into the atmosphere too.

Your Planet Earth is being plagued with so many detrimental things which mankind brings about by ignorance. This causes a denser and denser mist to Form which it is hard for us to penetrate to reach you.

There is no doubt Man can be his own worst enemy. Truth can stare him in the face, but he turns away from it, thus he loses that helping hand forward which could enable him to break free from that which binds him. If Man is to progress on a spiritual level, then he must rid himself of those unhealthy traits in his character which will not fail to create problems for him.

Remember, beloved ones, your loving Father wants nothing more than to see His children reap a fine harvest when their earth life is spent, from the good seeds they have planted. Good seeds sown are rich in the essence of God, for He blesses each and every one of them and thus they cannot fall to produce first class results which benefit one's soul enormously.

Strive always to fashion your lives on those things that can bring your soul what it needs to prosper. Your Father God yearns to see the flowering of your soul, for it lets Him know how well you are progressing to reach a higher scale of spirituality.

There are, alas, a great number on your Earth Plane who show no interest in the spiritual aspect of their being, thus the qualities they often portray do not make for sound growth. Many are so materially governed that nothing else concerns them. Sadly, they are not paving the way for their soul's entry into the greater world which must come about one day, and no one knows when that will be. It rests with God, when He sees fit to call you back home to Spirit.

Be wise and start preparing now for the greater life ahead. Search for knowledge to aid you. Spare time and thought on spiritual matters. This way, you keep in tune with such things.

Enjoy what the material offers, by all means. After all, such things are God's gift to you, but take care not to abuse them. Bear in mind, however, things of a materialistic nature can fade away, but that which holds spiritual quality remains forever, and from it one can derive the greatest and most lasting joy.

THOUGHTS ARE LIVING THINGS

How many of you realise your thoughts are living things which help or mar your progress. The majority of mankind, we fear, is not aware of how much potency they hold, which enables good or bad to form from them. The chaos you see today has been helped to come about by the careless way man has generated his thoughts. They are so often tainted with unkindness, greed for gain and power over others.

How joyful it would be to see Man's thoughts holding a more spiritual quality, which would help to light up the world, to thus create the right atmosphere, which it so needs to clear the prevailing darkness.

Dear children of God, you must try to remember you all have a responsibility to see that your Earth Planet is being cleansed of those things detrimental to its existence. If you do not take the trouble to play your part in this, you fail in your respect for God's wonderful creation, and thus in grace you fall in His sight.

They who play the game of life in the right manner pave the way for their soul's advancement. We cannot over-emphasise the fact that your development stems from the responsible way you run your lives, and that of the good you put into it. No being can expect to mature spiritually if they fail to work within the Great Spirit's laws. Time and time again we see so many of His children being led astray by ruthless ones who profess to know the answers to life. Sadly, more often than not, they are left in a vulnerable state which creates problems for them.

We tell you, Man cannot do better than to trust in what the good Master taught. Be a lamb within His fold, and you can be sure of being fed well with the knowledge you need. Those who follow in His footsteps will never be led astray.

Bear in mind, beloved ones, the pattern of your life rests entirely on you for its shape and colour. The threads you use to weave it come from your thoughts, words and deeds. If they are not of a benevolent kind then you cannot expect to create a pattern of beauty and finesse.

I trust the words I bring will aid you. I desire nothing more than to help Man progress on his evolutionary pathway, which is not easy when knowledge is thin on the ground.

THE KEY TO PROGRESSION

Many of you live in the shadows of doubt because you have not allowed the light of understanding to enter your lives, which leaves your soul dissatisfied, for it fails to receive what it needs to promote it forward.

The key to progression can only come through one's search for truth. Once you open the door to enlightenment, that detriment known as ignorance shall be overcome, thus making it possible For you to move Forward to gain what truly matters in life.

Far and wide, it is clearly shown how the material is being allowed to dominate Man's life. There is no doubt mankind is heading for disaster, because of greed for gain, amongst other things of a lower nature, which keeps Man on a low level of consciousness. Fulfilment from spiritual things is rarely given a chance to form an impression. They are cast aside as if of no importance, for Man is inclined to believe the material is the be-all and end-all of his existence, which he shall discover one day to be an illusion. Alas, regret will then trouble his mind for the time wasted on useless pursuits which provide no lasting gain or contentment, because they do not hold what his spirit calls for.

Learn to understand, beloved ones, that each and every one of you has a vital part to play in the Great Father's scheme of things. Do not jeopardise this by not flowing with the tide of life, or you could surely find yourselves being swept along by a current of uncertainty which denies you peace of mind, which is so important to good soul progress.

There may be times when you feel tested to the hilt by life's problems. Try to take them in your stride, knowing what is sent for you to endure comes for a purpose. We know from experience it is not easy to bear with good grace the sorrows and hardships of life that can leave one at a low ebb, but, dear children of God, one's experience of such things helps enormously in the awakening of our higher senses, where the seat of understanding dwells.

It is by tasting the bitter things of life that we are able to be of help to others in such circumstances. What is more, it enables us to gain an important ingredient which is good for the strengthening of our character.

There is no doubt that each and everyone of us is designing a pattern from our lifestyle, which helps to make up the great tapestry of life. Be then wise in the way this is taking shape if you want it to take pride of place. Remember, whatever you do shall not go unnoticed; plainly it will be seen.

May the words I speak speed you on to do what is right. Bear in mind the art of good living comes through knowledge of eternal truth where the key to progression can be yours.

THE VOICE OF THE SPIRIT

How many of you hearken to the voice of the Spirit that tries to lead you into the light of all that truly matters in life, whereby your soul might mature and so have the opportunity of rising to a higher dimension where a closer relationship with God can prevail. We know the pattern of many souls' lives fails to show beautiful shades of spirituality, due more often than not to a selfish life style. We cannot emphasise too strongly how important it is to give time and thought to spiritual matters, which can enable us to progress if we adhere by what they hold.

God wants His children freed from the shackles of ignorance, to thus make it possible for them to build their lives into something gratifying to see. Spiritual literature is not hard to find, if you are prepared to seek it. Once you allow it to influence your life, you will discover how invaluable it is. For one thing, you could gain a greater capacity of understanding which you might not otherwise experience.

The gems of life are, without doubt, truth, knowledge, and wisdom. You cannot advance towards the Godhead until you use them. They carry the power that can help you to ascend heavenward's.

Beloved ones, take time to learn the truth of the Spirit, and thus you shall find it amply rewards you. Furthermore, allow knowledge and wisdom to rank high in your lives, for this perfect twosome can light up your life, guiding your soul in a way which is sure to meet with God's approval. Try blending these things with that of love, peace, and goodwill, and you shall have the finest ingredients to encourage good wholesome growth which cannot fail to enhance your spirit.

Sadly, a goodly number of beings in your world are out of tune with life, thus making it difficult for them to receive the inspiration they need to help them out of the quandary they often find themselves in because of their lack of enlightenment. If they were only aware of the voice of the spirit which tries to teach them the right way to live, their life would be more harmonious.

Encourage the seeds of goodness to grow in the garden of your soul that they might blossom forth to emanate beauty which could encourage others to do likewise. Bear in mind, dear children of the Great Spirit, you all have a part to play in the great picture of life. See that the part you play brings joy to others.

THE RAIMENT OF YOUR SPIRIT

Each one of you is in the process of weaving the clothing that one day will dress your spirit. See then the threads you use are of the spiritual kind, which are strong and touched with gold.

The beauty that manifests from it will depend entirely on the way you live your lives, the colour shall show the rank of your spirituality. They who are working for the good of humanity can be sure of their raiment reflecting quality due to the fine threads woven in from the great work they do. Those who allow themselves to live their life in a useless fashion shall find it lacks colour and that of finesse.

So many of God's children waste their lives doing things of a fruitless nature which cannot possibly bring any profitable return to thus help in the maturing of their soul growth. We from Spirit World are often dismayed by those on the earth plane who treat spirituality as of no consequence. Souls such as these could be in for a rude awakening one day when God calls them back home to Spirit, because their lack of knowledge on spiritual matters would not have stood them in good stead and therefore they are likely to find themselves in a somewhat confusing situation unprepared for the change that takes place, which could prevent them from moving forward.

There is, we know, a tremendous need for enlightenment in your world. So many are going astray because they are without truth and knowledge to help them find direction in life. Man, however, must want to learn about the things that can aid him, if he chooses to close his mind against them then in ignorance he shall remain. You are the keeper of your own destiny. Whatever you choose to do will be your responsibility. You cannot blame God for what goes wrong in your lives. Freewill has been granted to you. It is therefore up to you to use it wisely.

So many beings fail to listen to the voice of reason which tries to help us see things in a more favourable light. No child of God can expect to make satisfactory progress by living in a narrow-minded way. They need to appreciate the fact that by adopting this attitude much is lost to them. God grants His children numerous opportunities to thus make it possible for them to gain a higher degree of spirituality. They who are wise shall see them for what they are and so make good use of them.

Think on the words I impart to you, beloved ones, for they can steer you in the right direction, and remember if the raiment of your spirit is to be of splendour, then you must choose with care the threads you are weaving in from what you do in your daily lives.

WAKE UP TO REALITY

There is without doubt a great number of beings who need to wake up to reality. Their way of life leaves much to be desired. In their ignorance, they fail to see where they are going wrong, and therefore are inclined to make mistake after mistake which just invites problems to complicate their lives.

Your world does not present a pleasant picture. For one thing, it shows too much darkness which is being created by the bad thoughts and deeds of many beings. Such ones are carrying out things which are far from in keeping with what God the Father wants to see in His picture of life.

Life, as you are experiencing it today cannot go on this way. Materialism is ranking too high, bringing more and more greed in its wake. This not only gives rise to aggression, but self-centredness also shows itself in plenty, for sadly, when greed enters the mind, thought and feeling for others often diminish. If this is not curtailed, mankind will head for disaster, where he shall be counting the cost of this unwise behaviour.

We mentors from the World of Spirit try our best to alert you to the danger signals which could be triggered off by over-stepping the mark but, more often than not, our words fall on stony ground.

The time is, however, approaching where mankind will have no choice but to wake up to reality. Happenings that take place shall topple materialism off its pedestal. The Aquarian Age will bring forth knowledge which spells truth in no uncertain terms. Much learning will be done, which will awaken the higher senses of man's mind which have been allowed to slumber for too long. God has been mocked and His Creation badly abused by Man's heartless behaviour.

Mankind would do well to bear in mind that all wrong must be paid for. This is one of the laws of life. If he continues to ignore the laws governing the universe, then he will learn a hard lesson.

Turn not away from truth, for it enables us to build a strong foundation from which sound development can stem. Let not your life be a wasted affair. Cultivate those things you know God would approve of. Inspiration will come if you use the right attitude of mind, and remember, beloved ones, every good seed you sow in life will flower in the garden or your heavenly home which you are building now by your thoughts and deeds.

THE GEMS OF LIFE

What are the gems of life, you may ask? They are, beloved ones, those spiritual values which all should use if they want their spirit to shine before God.

As one travels through life, opportunities arise where we are offered the chance to bring Spirituality into our lives, that we might derive benefit from the gems it holds. But, alas, not all of God's children are wise enough to see the value which lies there, and thus are inclined to dismiss it out of hand as something of little importance.

These unenlightened ones could find it difficult to flow with the tide of life when trials and tribulations confront them, because they would not have the insight to see how best to meet and overcome the things that come to test their spirit.

Free will, we know, is a God-given privilege which entitles us to play the game of life as we think fit, but one would do well to remember, should we play it with only materialism in mind, then the spiritual aspect of our being shall, without doubt, suffer neglect.

One's soul growth needs constant stimulation from that which bears the name of truth, knowledge and wisdom. What is more, our growth needs to be founded on good principles, which are not always taken into account when man's thoughts rest entirely on the material.

We know it is not easy to walk the spiritual pathway but, I tell you this, beloved ones, the reward at the end is truly well worth striving For. It is, however, a sad Fact of life that a large majority of God's children prefer to travel the path of materialism where emphasis is placed on satisfying the lower self with what it craves for.

But, the time will surely come when these souls must pass to another dimension, where worldly things are not considered to be of importance. Thus the awakening to the truth of what is revealed to them could be quite a revelation, because they shall be faced with changing their outlook if they want to progress to the realms of enchantment where the more noble ones dwell.

The wise beings of the world are they who look beyond the material, knowing there is much to gain by seeing things from a spiritual point of view. They are aware too of the fact that all that is based on spirit is lasting, in every sense of the word

We ask you to open your heart and mind to the glory of God, to thus allow Him to draw close to you where all that He stands For might be expressed through your being For others to see and so take wisdom from.

THE PATH TO HAPPINESS

The path to happiness is not one you find by easy methods. You must earn the right to discover it, by giving to others what you would wish for yourself, which, in one word, is 'love'.

They who allow pure unselfish love to flow from their being to help others in the world are working in harmony with God, and this cannot Fail to bring a deep sense of satisfaction to their soul.

Alas, as we view the world in which you live, it shows man is not contributing much in the way of love. Numerous souls are living a self centred way of life, giving little or no thought to others. The pattern of your world looks drab indeed, because the threads that are being woven in from the lives of many are not of spiritual quality, and thus show no brightness of colour.

Those whose life is based on selfishness and greed will be in for a rude awakening when they are called back home to Spirit one day. No favourable light shall surround them and, what is more, they shall see themselves as they truly are as they face the truth of their fruitless life.

So much could man do to improve the conditions of the earth plane, if he would only try to find understanding in his heart for his fellow-men. Pain and suffering could then be avoided, war and strife need come no more.

If mankind would only put into practice that which could clear your world of the darkness that prevails, what a change in the atmosphere there would be. Man's spiritual education should rank high in his life. Foolish is he who casts it aside, because he thinks it is of no consequence. Man can often be his own worst enemy by rocking the foundation of his growth through his negative thoughts and actions.

I tell you this, beloved ones, so much could you achieve in the way of progress, if you would only see the logic in the words I speak. My main aim is to guide you on to that path to happiness, which is sound and progressive, that you might finally reach the centre of the power governing the universe, where you can experience in all glory the strength of God's love. No greater joy could one desire than that of knowing they are so near to Him who is the Creator of their being.

OPEN YOUR MIND

Children of the Great Spirit open your minds to the truth God sees fit to send you to help you gain enlightenment. God in His wisdom knows His children must learn from every angle or life, to thus allow them to grow in the way His dream calls for. If we avoid the knowledge of life then we have only ourselves to blame if our soul drifts into a state of stagnation.

One should constantly endeavour to feed the mind with the food of the spirit to keep their soul nourished with the goodness it contains. Man has no excuse for not doing this, it is so easy to do and can be fitted in any time during the course of his daily life. We teachers from Spirit World try to educate you to the way of the spirit, but this can be difficult at times when minds are blocked against us.

Mankind would do well to bear in mind that when his soul is released from the body one day what spiritual achievement will it have made to thus prepare it for the journey into the greater world. Those who have been sensible in the way they have conducted their lives shall find their soul has no difficulty in adjusting to the next life. On entry to that fair land it shall find a host of good things which joy can be taken from, because the soul would have earnt the right to the glory or them.

Those who turn away from the truth of the spirit do not know what they are missing. Foolishly, they think they know best and therefore shall not find it easy to acclimatise to the conditions which call for progression.

Take heed of what I say in truth. I bring you the knowledge that can help you to grow in awareness, thus enabling you to gain a clearer understanding of life and its purpose, standing you in good stead for whatever life brings your way. The power of the spirit can be yours to aid you if you learn how to use it wisely. Never abuse the power of God, or you will find the strength behind its purpose shall surely wane.

Many times in your lives you will no doubt find situations inviting you to express what knowledge you have gained. How helpful this will prove to be to others who seek the truth you hold, because you have wisely kept an open mind to thus receive that literature of that which truly matters.

Blessed indeed are they who live their lives in accordance with what the Father God wants to see carried out, making it therefore possible for their spirit to join Him in the fullness of time.

THE ETERNAL QUEST

The search for the truth of life can be a somewhat complicated affair because the knowledge one meets might conflict with what we were taught to believe. But one must reason with what comes to light in the course of our searching, for who knows what pearls of wisdom we may find.

Too many souls hinder their progress by holding a narrow-minded point of view, but they would do well to bear in mind that this could prevent them from learning what could be to their advantage.

If one is to discover the true facts of life, then patience and perseverance are the two companions we need to help us in our quest. A great deal can be gained by leaning toward a spiritual source, for the seeds of truth are to be found in good supply there, which the Father God wants His children to partake of.

However, we must remember that one may not always find the answers to that which we are seeking, because God, in His wisdom, could decide we are not ready to receive that which we want revealed. Our level of consciousness determines what truth and knowledge should be fed to us, and He, and He alone, knows how much we can digest to thus help our spiritual growth.

The pattern of one's life shows the weakness and the strength of those threads that are being woven in from the process of our learning. Therefore, I say to you, see that the threads you use are strong, knowing they come from knowledge which you have found to be fundamentally sound in every way.

Your world teems with souls who are unaware of the fact that the pattern forming from their lifestyle will indeed show whether or not it is based on spirituality. Those whose lives are, shall be weaving in threads of gold which cannot fail to shine for all to see. But, alas, they who allow their lifestyle to be one that is wholly materialistic are in for rude awakening, for the pattern they are weaving shall show a distinctive lack of that which the Father wants to see, if it is to fit perfectly in life's great tapestry.

We, who are mentors, try to feed your mind with truth that you must face if you are to progress on the path of spiritual unfoldment. There is much to learn, and so the eternal quest for truth and knowledge goes on until we reach the end of all time, which no one as yet has any notion of.

One thing we can be sure of, and that is, in God's good time, we shall reach a clear understanding of what life's purpose is all about.

THE LIGHT OF REASON

We know many of you search for the light of reason to help you see and thus understand why the world in which you live holds so much turmoil when it is thought there is a God of love who is responsible for the Kingdom He has made. But, I say to you, it is not God's desire that you His children should live in a state of adversity. Man has brought much upon himself over a long period of time which is working against him because the laws of life have been greatly defied. This has created disharmony which is causing a marked decline in the way beings in your world live.

But this cannot go on. Love, peace and harmony must be allowed to flow through your life so that you might find attunement with the Infinite One. What is more, man needs to learn how to commune with his fellow-beings in a just and caring way to prevent animosity arising, which more often than not stems from a lack of understanding which can lead to bitterness and contempt.

You could all do so much to bring light into your world to help dispel the darkness that prevails by carrying out acts of kindness, showing more generosity, goodwill and compassion for those less fortunate than yourself.

Sadly, it is true that a large majority of God's children show little or no interest in searching for enlightenment, nor do they want to know how to make their world a better place to live in. So many go through life in a most irresponsible way, caring not for what they should be achieving to promote the spiritual side of their being.

Bear in mind, God places before His children the means to help them rise above the lower conditions of the earth plane, which can weigh the soul down to a low level of existence where it could fail to see the light which guides the more enlightened ones on to gain what their souls need.

Truth and wisdom are without doubt the two main key factors of life that can open the door of enlightenment where one gains insight into the reality of life, thus helping one to become aware of those values which should be important to you. I therefore urge you to seek both these gems of spirituality, for without them your progress will prove to be unsatisfactory. Look upon them as a light that help you to see a clearer picture of life and its purpose, thus giving you the incentive to move towards the path which leads to greater things.

THE VOICE OF LOVE

Take time, beloved ones, to listen to the Voice of Love that speaks from the heart of you, the core of your being, and you will find guidance forthcoming. You cannot mistake the Voice of Love, it holds the gentleness of peace to soothe one's troubled spirit when faced with the problems of life.

Many, it seems, are not given to listening to God, the Voice of Love. If they did so, their lives would be based on good principles, which alas are seen to be lacking.

Spirituality is the jewel that should be in every soul's life. Nothing can beat it for value. It is of prime importance to our progress, without it one's spirit cannot shine before God.

Spiritual education ideally should start at a very young age when the mind is more receptive. The seeds of knowledge planted therein are given a chance to grow more freely then without the clutter of the many earthly things adult minds are obliged to deal with whilst living in a material world. However, excuses must not be made in this respect. Room for knowledge can always be found, no matter what else is housed in the mind. Knowledge can act as our salvation in time of need; it enables us to become aware of the truth of life which sets us free from ignorance.

Sadly, a goodly number of souls drift through lift unenlightened, knowing not where they are heading. This invariably has a profound effect on their spirit, for it stands to be neglected simply because no wise catering is being done to feed its needs.

Man tends to overlook the fact that his spiritual growth is the most important part of his life. By being careless about this he does his spirit a grave injustice, lessening its chance of promotion to those realms of splendour which offer so much, to thus speed one's spirit heaven wards.

Beloved ones, keep company with your spirit. Treat it with respect, help it to gain truth, knowledge and wisdom from the opportunities of life which God sends for us to learn from. Remember, your spirit is trying to reach the light of Him Most High. Do not prevent this by failing to minister to its needs, or regret will be yours. All too often we see beings pampering the lower self, whilst the higher self is forgotten. Believe me, they have much to learn.

Those who are not spiritually motivated would do well to ponder upon my words. My aim is to help souls face the truth of what truly matters, so that they might consider taking the path of righteousness.

I beseech thee to take time out for God, Whose desire it is to guide you. You are His children and He, your loving Father, wants to see you moving in the right direction, to thus receive one day the good things He has planned.

SERVICE

They who take on the role of serving God must remember they are in a position of trust, and therefore should see that the work they carry out for Him is done in a responsible manner. Far too many serve Him with the wrong attitude of mind, which makes a mockery of what they do. The Great Spirit wants to see an element of genuineness running through those who serve Him, so that He can place His trust in them without concern.

We who work for God in a high capacity know how necessary it is for Him to have workers He can fully depend upon when special missions need to be carried out. Strength of character must be proven in every conceivable way. God leaves nothing to chance where the working out of His Plan is concerned, thus you can be sure privileged roles are only allocated to those who have earned His respect by their effort to reach a high standard of spirituality.

There are, without doubt, a goodly number of souls in your world who are trustworthy workers who are blessed by the Great Father for what they do. They are the backbone of society who help to keep the light of goodness shining through. Without such beings your world would lack the strong threads of stability they weave into the pattern of life.

One can assist God in many ways. Tasks waiting to be carried out are numerous, but you must be sure your heart is in what you do for Him. This is essential if you are to give of your best; nothing would be gained by working in a half-hearted fashion.

Service can indeed be all inspiring, helping one to create a wealth of betterment for others to derive benefit from. To serve is truly a noble thing and the more you serve, and thus give of yourself in service, the closer to God you become.

Your world is full of wanting souls needing guidance in one way or another, and so often they look to those who have acquired knowledge of the true and trusted kind to help them. It is therefore so important that the assistance they are given borders on what is right for them. One must bear in mind that all have different needs, depending on their circumstances. Servers hold a responsible position and the foundation of this must not be rocked by allowing a careless attitude to take hold over what they do.

Beloved ones, I would have you know the Great Father is ever watchful and thus is very aware of how His Creation is taking shape. We therefore must let Him see that we, His children, are abiding by what He expects of us, so that His dream for us works out in accordance with His plans.

Be then faithful to your Creator and serve Him well in whatever way you can, thus by doing so you are playing a vital part in His great scheme of things which shall, without doubt, bring joy to His heart.

THE WAY OF THE SPIRIT

Truth, knowledge, and wisdom enlighten us to the way of the Spirit, and thus we must try to encompass them as we travel life's way. Sadly, it appears a vast majority of beings are far from interested in trying to educate themselves with spiritual matters essential to their soul development.

The Father God yearns to see His children making headway in their spiritual learning to thus prepare their soul for the greater things ahead. Such a grand range of opportunities awaits those who are earning the right to embrace them. God never limits what can be gained. It is therefore up to us to strive purposefully towards the things which can offer us so much in the way of advancement. If we fail to make the effort, then we have only ourselves to blame for what little we receive or achieve.

We mentors from Spirit side of life try to light the lamp of truth in your lives to help you see the way forward, but alas many shun what we do, which of course is their prerogative, and thus we must respect this.

One of the saddest facts of life is that ignorance continues to reign supreme, which is why the world is in such upheaval. Try as we may, we do not find it easy to break through the darkness brought about by Man's unhealthy way of living. But, the light of God which we carry with us is strong, and is our weapon against the Forces of a lower nature which try to prevent us From bringing enlightenment for one and all to gain from. Once truth and knowledge are instilled into Man's mind, then what is revealed can guide him to do what is right.

They who walk the way of the Spirit can be sure of heading in the right direction. It might not be an easy path to tread, but spiritual maturity, amongst other things, is to be gained, allowing one's soul to reach a state of consciousness where the presence of God leaves one in no doubt of the greatness of Him.

The Divine Spirit of Love wants to see His children grow spiritually strong from lessons learnt, which He knows can stand us in good stead for greater roles He wants us to play in the universal picture of life. We therefore must try not to disappoint Him by adopting a contrary attitude. We shall only spite ourselves if we do, which would be rather foolish when our Father offers so much to help us obtain roles of prominence.

Remember, beloved ones, you cannot go wrong if you walk the way of the Spirit. It leads us to gain greater understanding, thus opening up our awareness to the truth of life, which one needs if they are to progress.

May the love and peace of God fill your being, and may you forever walk in the radiance of His light.

THE PICTURE OF LIFE

All of creation has a part to play in the great Picture of Life and God, Who directs this, wants to see it holding the quality He planned. Therefore, we, His children, must try to play our part in a responsible manner to thus help Him achieve what His heart so desires.

They who act irresponsibly disrupt the rhythm running through it, which creates an atmosphere of unrest. Harmony is vital in bringing about good results, if this is disturbed then the foundation of what is being carried out weakens in the process.

Your Father God has put much time and effort into what He has created, which His wondrous mind saw fit to contrive and, although you may not understand the reason or the purpose behind some of creation, you can be sure that all have a part to play in His scheme of things.

They who are on a low level of consciousness cannot possibly see things in the same light as those on a higher level. They would not have that knowledge allowing them to gain insight into those perplexing things which appear to have no rhyme or reason. Knowledge holds the key to enlightenment which all should be searching for if they want to grow in awareness, to thus appreciate more fully the purpose of life.

Each and every child of the Great Father is responsible for their words and actions, which, if not of the right kind, can spoil the beauty of God's picture by creating dark shadows where light should be. Respect what I have said, it is important that you do so, for your progress, too, depends on it.

The Father has blessed us all with the gift of creativity so that we, too, might bring forth things of usefulness and of beauty to add to what He has made. Sadly, many of His children do not use this gift in the way they should. In the wake of their ignorance, they often create only trouble and strife which does nothing to enhance their role in life. Indeed, they cast themselves on a low level which is not a pleasing sight to see.

If you want to shine in the Picture of Life, then you must earn the right to do so. Important roles must be strived for. Time and time again you might have to struggle to win such a role, but remember, beloved ones, victory is sweet when mastering defeat, and thus you gain the satisfaction of knowing you are moving towards gaining that of stardom, which your Father God wants to see all His children achieve.

TRAVEL WITH WISDOM

As we travel through life we can do no better than to let wisdom guide us. So few think in this way, and therefore find they become lost on the way. Sadly, wisdom is not used enough in your world, hence the reason for the problems existing today. Many beings find themselves in difficult situations, mainly because they fail to allow wisdom to direct them.

Man would do well to see this as a most valuable tool that can serve him well in all areas of his life. It also provides that which is needed to enable one's soul to reach maturity. The wise man knows how to conduct his life. He sees clearly the way to go, thus avoiding the obstacles which could obstruct his progress. He does this by listening to the voice of reason and by acting with caution when dealing with the harrowing things of life which try to defeat him.

Many souls are impetuous. They rush into things without thinking, which, more often than not, breeds trouble for them. Wise beings try to avoid this. They look before they leap, thus saving themselves from unwelcome come-backs which are likely to happen if one takes a careless line of conduct. True, God has blessed us, His children, with free-will, and therefore we are at liberty to do as we see fit with our lives. But, beloved ones, let us not be unwise by behaving irresponsibly, or we stand to deprive our soul of what it needs to stimulate sound growth.

There is joy to be gained in knowing we are trying to perfect our soul with the correct method of treatment which God would approve. By paying attention to what truly matters in life, one can be sure their soul will return back home to Spirit one day in good shape and form to thus receive the opportunity to enter those realms holding all one's heart could desire.

They who make the effort to learn the true facts of life shall indeed be helped by those higher minds who reside in the glory of God. Those in the early stage of enlightenment are fed carefully the food of knowledge, thus making it easier to digest. It must be understood that all God's children are at a different stage of evolution, and therefore need to be given only what they are comfortable with.

Those who are advanced in their spiritual education would be fed greater knowledge, thus allowing them to attune with souls who hold the key to mastership. Wisdom is at the very root of what they carry out, which enables them to serve God in a high capacity. Wisdom is a gem one cannot afford to be without if we are to reach the summit of spirituality. Bear this in mind, beloved ones, and your progress will be safeguarded.

THE ESSENCE OF ALL LIFE

Alas, so many tend to overlook the fact that the Great Spirit is the essence of all life, and indeed in all we survey. Without Him, there would be nothing.

This lack of understanding of the Father God is shown all too clearly in the way His Creation is abused. Man should try to take time out to view closely His work of art, thus by doing so, he might become that bit more aware of how much thought and care has gone into it. Perhaps realise, too, how miraculous the working of His great mind is.

Sadly, in this day and age, which has become one of rush and tear, not enough time is spent on the things which matter. Man's mind is so full of the material that the spiritual tends to take a back seat in his life. Peace and harmony cannot exist in a world where too much materialism holds sway. Trouble and strife breed in the wake of it, for when Man fails to raise his consciousness to a higher level, lower influences take advantage of this and thus creep in to create disruption.

They who are content to live on a low level of consciousness lose out on so much. For one thing, their soul is not gaining the growth it needs to reach maturity. Living on this level is indeed fruitless, for nothing worthwhile is achieved from it.

We beseech thee to live your lives in a sensible way, so that regret will not be yours to experience one day. Foolish are they who allow themselves to be bound by ignorance. No soul need stay restricted by this. Knowledge awaits all who are prepared to seek it. Guidance will always be forthcoming from Spirit side of life when we see you are trying to move forward into the light of understanding. Our desire is to share what we know with you from our learning, that you might find it helps you to grow spiritually strong, to thus enable you to reach those higher planes awaiting those who are earning the right to enter therein.

Bear in mind, beloved ones, you all have a spark of the divine light within you linking you with God. Alas, so many suppress this by a selfish lifestyle. If only they would fan this light into a flame by doing good in the world, what a difference it would make to their being. For one thing, their aura would be one of brightness, thus showing they are allowing God's light to shine through, which He wants His children to do so much, because it shows Him they care.

Build your lives on those things that bring advancement to your soul. You can then be sure your spirit is gaining that which it needs to find oneness with God, Who is the essence of all life.

GOD'S DREAM

Mankind must learn to understand the fact that God's dream is one He wants to see materialise in all glory. Sadly, His children are not helping Him to achieve this. So many are thwarting His plan in a way that brings sorrow to His heart.

Throughout the ages, mankind has given little time or thought to their Father God, or indeed to the wonder of His Creation which, if man studied more, he would thus see and perhaps appreciate the work that has gone into it which the Father's creative mind first had to devise before bringing into being.

We from the higher side of life are very aware of God's aspirations, and from time to time are given privileged glimpses into the golden things He has in store. But they shall not be granted to the world until the Great Spirit is assured of His children's readiness to receive them.

Believe me, mankind has much learning to do if he wants to grow spiritually strong to thus receive respect from God. Disruptive behaviour, greed, and lack of loving kindness are things the Father God deeply frowns upon, for they cause harm and discontent which does not make for pleasant living.

The humble beings of life are more likely to move closer to God where their soul shall find a place to flower in His heart We ask you to look at your lives with careful scrutiny and thus note the things which are not in keeping with your spiritual welfare. Should this be lacking in the food of the spirit, we beseech thee to put it right or your soul's development will suffer the consequences.

Beautiful is the spirit or those who cultivate fine traits in their character from the good they do in life. This is not hard to do if you allow your heart to hold the qualities it should.

We know there are many temptations in life which try to draw one away from goodness but, beloved ones, we say be wise, be strong, and allow nothing to prevent you from going forward on to the path of spiritual progression which leads to many wonderful things which your Father God holds in store for you. All He asks is that you at least try to educate yourselves with knowledge of eternal truth that you might progress to higher states of consciousness to thus gain the prizes of life which await they who qualify for them.

Beloved ones, in the hustle and bustle of your lives, fail not to remember God's dream. Help Him to bring it to fruition by living and working in accordance with His plan. Improve the state of the world by bringing more love, peace, and harmony into it. Be true and faithful to Him Who is your Father and the Maker of your being, and do not forget that He is the power behind all you behold.

THE CHAIN OF LIFE

We are all linked together in the great chain of life that connects us to the Father God. This cannot be severed unless the Father sees fit to bring this about. However, the links of the chain can be weakened or strengthened by the way we live our lives. Therefore, it is well to remember to be cautious in word and deed. If they are not of a benevolent kind, this will surely show, for our link in the chain shall be without lustre, thus looking comparatively dull compared with those that are being polished with the milk of human kindness which other souls are expressing in their lives.

Try always to keep your link strengthened by keeping in close contact with God. One can do this in many ways. Serving Him is a grand thing to do. Channels for mediumship and healing are always needed. Bringing truth and knowledge to bear upon those locked in ignorance, from what you have gained, is also a worthy service.

Always one can find a service to perform in some shape or Form to help another and it matters not how small the deed is. It is the good you do that counts in the sight of God. He gains much pleasure From seeing your links shining brightly from the benevolent acts you carry out.

Numerous souls live in a way the Great Father frowns upon. Their lives centre only on them. These ones have much to learn if they are to evolve satisfactorily. The heart of beings who are self-centred is cold; they do not radiate light and beauty as do those who give generously of themselves to bring comfort and joy to others by that method of sharing and caring. Souls such as these experience a warm inner glow which they take contentment from. This cannot be said of those who show a one-track mind where their thoughts dwell entirely on their own lives.

Thus we can only hope and pray their minds shall one day register the truth of how selfishly they live. Many beings in your world need to master unhealthy traits in their character if they are to advance spiritually. Until they are ready to do this, help cannot be forthcoming from Spirit side of life.

We should all take stock of our lives from time to time, to thus make sure it is taking good shape. One could find a correction needs to be made here and there where we have been careless. No one is perfect, and therefore we are likely to make mistakes which we should learn to rectify if our character is to grow in strength. God is a loving Father and understands our human weaknesses, but we must try to avoid repeating errors made or a price will have to be paid.

Beloved ones, do not fail your Father God by letting Him see your link in the chain of life has weakened from wrong thought and deeds. Help it to sparkle by endeavouring to prosper spiritually, thus in doing so you will move closer to Him to thus experience the brilliance of His light and the warmth of His love, which without doubt can exhilarate one's spirit.

68

THE MASTERS

There is, we know, a yearning with some of you to learn about the Masters, and thus it is my pleasure and privilege to convey to you what knowledge I hold of them.

These very wise and enlightened souls have earned their high ranking status through long, dedicated service to God, and by gaining a wealth of knowledge from numerous lifetimes, some of which proved to be arduous indeed.

Patience and perseverance and that of steadfastness were, by their very nature, the things they needed to help them win through. The desire to experience all aspects of life was of prime importance, for they knew if they were to be of service to their fellow-beings then true understanding must come about in a way that would be right in the eyes of God.

These paragons of the universe are truly the most humble of beings, who are bathed in the light of the Divine One. We who reside in the dimensions beyond the fourth are able to commune with them on their fine wavelength, because our level of consciousness makes it possible for us to do so, as does the nature of our work, which is partly to do with feeding knowledge to humanity.

Love and compassion reign high in the hearts of the Masters and oft-times they descend to the earth plane to walk unseen amongst you, trying to bring light to your troubled world, which increasingly darkens by mankind's senseless behaviour, which is breeding so much strife and discontent.

Their task is by no means an easy one, as they battle with a force bent on destroying, but nothing shall daunt their strong and courageous spirits, for they have learnt how to control those things which are detrimental to progress.

No eye below their dimension has seen their dwelling-place; the radiance of the light that shines there is far too bright for beings of lower spheres to enter into. However, the Masters can and do visit regions beneath them by lowering their vibration to thus bring teachings to bear upon those who dwell therein.

We in Spirit World eagerly await their visitations. They bring with them such love, peace and gentleness of spirit which fill our souls with bliss and we feel so richly blessed knowing we are learning from them. The aura surrounding their being is indeed breathtaking to see.

One such Master is the Christ Spirit who holds us enthralled by the sheer beauty that manifests from Him, which lights up a desire in our hearts to be like Him. But, we are aware of our imperfections which we must work on before such a prime position, calling for qualities of godliness, can be entrusted to us, who work on a less superior level.

They who want to reach the summit of spirituality must be prepared to face many tests of life. One cannot afford to be faint-hearted if this goal is to be achieved. Only those strong in character shall win through to rise heavenward's.

The strengthening of one's character can come from taking on roles of a spiritual nature which call for sacrifice, amongst other things, but this must rest with you, dear children of the Great Spirit. We mentors can only point the way, the choice must be yours as to whether or not you accept our guidance.

The Masters are closely involved with God's Plan of things and therefore work on a high level. All tasks carried out are done with the utmost care. They hold an extremely responsible position which demands faithfulness to their Maker. But, the Great Spirit in His wisdom knows these His trusted ones would do nothing to jeopardise what He wants to achieve. They have been tested to the hilt, thus proving their worth.

Blessed indeed are they who are trying to follow the Path of the Masters. Although not an easy one to tread, by any means, it is an all-inspiring one which holds promise and the opportunity to move close to the Godhead, which is a dream many hold.

PATIENCE IS A VIRTUE

Be patient in your search for truth and you shall find He who loves you will guide you to that which your soul seeks. The Great Father of mankind appreciates His children's quest for knowledge to help them understand the whys and wherefores of life. But, beloved ones, truth cannot all be revealed in a moment of time, the mind could not grasp it. It is through experiences of trials and tribulations one learns the true facts of life whereby enlightenment comes to those ready to receive it. One must remember, each and every child of God is at a different stage of evolution, thus the soul's need must be met accordingly. That which is right for one could be wrong for another, therefore the Great Father metes out only that which He knows His children are capable of receiving.

Be not anxious if your standard of learning does not measure up to another's. It could simply mean you might not have reached that level of consciousness whereby they have acquired more knowledge. But, beloved ones, all can advance, it is God's will that you do so. Just strive steadily on and try to accomplish what you know is good for the growth of your soul.

The Great Father is ever watchful, calculating His children's every need, and although there are those who are blind to His light which guides them, and many are deaf to the words He speaks, the Father in His wisdom knows all must learn the truth of life at some stage in their evolution. His plans for us are infinite and perfect in every way, but we must try to live in harmony with His scheme of things so that we might be in tune with the great orchestra of life.

Remember, dear children of the Great Spirit, patience is a virtue that should be practised in your life. Nothing can be gained by trying to achieve too much too soon, it only complicates progress. The wise men of old were patient souls who took time to learn the wisdom of life, and thus, by doing so, gained much from it. You, too, could try to follow their example and, like them, you would surely find the journey to God proves to be truly worthwhile.

TRUTH

All truth is stored in the heart of God, but if one is prepared to seek what He holds then He will gladly release it to help you gain mastery over ignorance. A vast number of residents in your world muddle their way through life without an inkling of what life is about and this creates problems for them because, without truth to guide them, they live in the shadow of doubt.

They who hold truth shall not fall victim to that which could hinder their progress, for they know they can conquer whatever tries to disconcert them. Truth is the realisation of knowing one has gained insight into what the soul needs to take it further up the stairway of life.

Wise indeed are they who seek to learn the whys and wherefores of life which can broaden one's outlook and help one to see how important the search for truth can be, for no soul progresses satisfactorily without it.

Truth frees us from the shackles of life that can bind us to false reality which weakens the foundation of our growth, thus leaving one in a vulnerable situation against the forces which come to test the innermost strength of our being. We must therefore prize truth highly for it can nourish and sustain that which the Father wants to see grow and unfold in spiritual beauty.

We from the higher side of life are very aware of those in your world who are drifting along with no sense of direction as to where they should be heading to gain fulfilment for their soul. We therefore seek help from those of you who are knowledgeable of such things that you might help us in our work by trying to guide these wanting ones you may meet in the course of your life with words of truth to thus enable them to see and understand what steps they should be taking to bring about a more steady forward looking way of life.

Blessed are they who help another as they travel forth on life's way, for they shall find God's touch brings a warmth of satisfaction to their heart.

GUIDELINES

We all need guidance in our lives to help us evolve in a satisfactory way. So I offer you guidelines which have proved to serve me well, thus enabling me to progress to higher levels of learning where soul maturity can be gained. I trust you, too, might derive benefit from them, as I proceed to enlighten you.

Be ever true to the Maker of your being. Do nothing you know would be against the laws He sets for us to live by, or you could disturb the very essence of His Plan. Remember, you are playing a role in His great scheme of things, see then you are carrying it out in a responsible manner.

Your Father God wants to see His children spreading joy and happiness in the world, not bitterness and hatred which appears to be increasing all the time because Man fails to master ignorance, which sadly weakens his soul growth. Bear in mind, beloved ones, what you sow in your earthly life will be the harvest you reap in the next one. Should you therefore be sowing seeds that are poor from, say, a selfish lifestyle, then you shall have nothing to gather in and the prospects of your moving to spheres holding promise and delight could be extremely slim indeed, for you would not have earned the right to do so.

How many of you take the trouble to count the blessings God has bestowed upon you, rarely is He thanked for the good things He sends into your lives. Many are quick to blame Him when things go wrong, which is unfair and totally unjust. God is a loving Father who would not harm His children in any way. The problems that arise in our lives usually come about by the fact that we are not always living in accordance with His laws. Many difficulties are experienced because they come as tests to try our spirit, which one should try to accept with good grace, for they can help us to graduate to higher levels of consciousness.

Alas, a goodly number of beings have this theory where they truly believe there is nothing beyond the earth plane, thus they drift through life in a somewhat irresponsible way, satisfying their lower self with things that do not even hold a spark of spirituality. What a surprise they shall receive when the time comes for them to move into the next dimension. Alas, their soul will show the mark of what's been denied it, and thus its distorted growth shall not be a pleasant sight to see.

They who want to look forward to the greater things of life should wake up to the fact that soul progression, and what comes from it, must be worked for. Nothing of spiritual value is given to any being until they have made the efforts to earn it. Those of you who are moving towards the Godhead through the light you have drawn to you from your desire to reach the summit of spirituality, shall indeed find guidance forthcoming from the

Paragons of the Universe, because they see the sincerity that lies within your heart, and thus with the blessing of the Father they are only too happy to aid you.

The greatness of one's soul can only come about by what we put into life. It is a wonderful sight to behold when Man's soul is made beautiful by that of service. Beloved ones, allow my words of wisdom to take root in your lives that they might influence you to do what is right. Remember to feed your soul with the fine food of the Spirit, which is based on knowledge. Show love and loving kindness to others. Be thoughtful, be true. Share and care with the right attitude of mind. Allow no thought of selfishness and greed or that of jealousy to corrupt the good you try to achieve.

Furthermore, let your mind rest on service where others could be helped by what you do. Perhaps a tall order, we know, but this is the only sure way of making sound wholesome progress which helps to create more light in your world. Last, but by no means least, take time to meditate in your daily lives, to thus allow the presence of God to draw near where His love and His peace can bring balm to your soul, thus helping to banish those doubts and fears which can so plague us when that gem of enlightenment is missing from one's life.

Meditation also opens the door of inspiration which can influence us to bring forth that of value which could be used to help humanity in some shape or form.

COUNT YOUR BLESSINGS

Ye who have found the way to God should count your blessings for your life shall prove to be a rewarding one where the door of opportunity opens to you inviting you to join forces with those beings of the light whose pleasure it shall be to guide and instruct you in that which God wants you to do.

But let us not forget those who have yet to reach this level of consciousness where the path to God is clearly seen. Souls such as these live in the shadows of life where the light of truth is blocked from their view. Thus, we must help to remove this restriction by showing them how to move forward in a sure and steady way.

No child of God should feel life is without purpose, because His plan for us all is truly wonderful to see. But we must learn to strive steadily on to reach the goal He sets us, so that we might prove worthy for the part He wants us to play in the great picture of life. Many of you have been blessed with spiritual gifts to use in accordance with His plans, therefore I say to you, count your blessings, for you have a privileged role to carry out in His scheme of things.

But do not forget, beloved ones, to use these gifts wisely. They who respect their worth and sincerely use them for the good of mankind shall indeed earn the jewel of distinction which God shall bestow upon them one day.

Never doubt the importance of work carried out for God. All that you achieve will be noted by Him and thus credited to you. I therefore say to those of you who are proving your worth, go forth with a joyful heart knowing you are shedding light to the world by your effort to inspire and uplift and comfort humanity.

DEDICATION

I dedicate this book to my Spirit Guide Pharaoh who's teachings hold a wealth of meaning to aid mankind. also to my late friend Teresa Doherty who gave me unfailing support in my work for spirit which I am deeply grateful for.

Teresa wrote the foreword to this book and my first book Teachings of Infinite Wisdom back in 1993.

May Clark